Guilty Until Proven Innocent

Guilty Until Proven Innocent

Elizabeth M. Schulz

Clear Mind Press

LEGAL

Guilty Until Proven Innocent
© Elizabeth M. Schulz
Published by Clear Mind Press
2023 Alice Springs, Australia

ISBN: 978-0-6458887-2-0

Cover design: Clear Mind Press
Back cover text: Margaret Allen
Photos cover: Author's collection
Photo front: Author's collection
Photos interior: Author's collection
Drawings interior: Author's collection
Portrait of the Author: Maria Ames

All rights reserved. Except as permitted under the Australian Copyright Act 1968 (for example, fair dealing for study, research, criticism or review), no part of this book may be reproduced, stored in a retrieval system, communicated or transmitted in any form or by any means without prior written permission.

All inquiries should be made to the publisher.
info@clearmindpress.com
https://www.clearmindpress.com

CONTENTS

LEGAL iv
ACKNOWLEDGEMENT viii
ILLUSTRATION 1 ix
FOREWORD x
INTRODUCTION xiv

1 | Germans in South Australia Before World War One 1

Map 1 16

Map 2 17

Table 1 18

Table 2 19

Map 3 20

2 | J.F.W. Schulz and Family Before World War Two 21

Illustration 2 37

Illustration 3 38

CONTENTS

Illustration 4   39

Illustration 5   40

3 | South Australia: Germans Between the Wars   41

Illustration 6   63

Illustration 7   64

4 | J. F. W. Schulz: Internment in World War Two   65

5 | Release: What Happened to Schulz?   92

6 | In Retrospect: A Summary of the Issues   101

Illustration 8   105

Illustration 9   106

Illustration 10   107

Appendix A   108

Appendix B   109

Appendix C   110

Appendix D   111

CONTENTS

Appendix E 112

Appendix F 113

Appendix G 114

Appendix H 115

Appendix I 116

Appendix J 117

7 | Bibliography 118

8 | Tables, maps and illustrations 129

9 | Apendices 131

ABOUT THE AUTHOR 132
ABOUT THE BOOK 134

ACKNOWLEDGEMENT

I would like to thank Ms Margaret Allen, Lecturer, Department of History, Salisbury College of Advanced Education, Mr. George Smith and Ms Mara Seaton, Australian Archives, Collinswood, and Rev. Philip A. Scherer Lutheran Archives, North Adelaide, for all the assistance given to me.

ILLUSTRATION 1

FOREWORD

When Liz Schulz researched and wrote this thesis in 1987, she had a burning desire to discover why her grandfather, Johann Friedrich Wilhelm Schulz (1883- 1964), had been interned for three years and under government labor controls for another year, during World War Two.

J.F.W. Schulz was an Australian and a British subject, being born two years after his parents had migrated to South Australia from Germany. Until his arrest and detention on 13 December 1940 under the provisions of the National Security Act (1939), he had always been seen as a loyal and well-respected member of his local community in the Barossa Valley in South Australia. Schulz was accused of attending Nazi party meetings and of keeping Nazi propaganda material in his home, and thus being an enemy of the state. He was detained at Wayville and subsequently at Tatura and Loveday internment camps, along with others of German, Italian and Japanese descent.

J.F.W. Schulz always maintained his innocence saying he had never been a threat to national security. In fact he had supported the war against Hitler's Germany and had worked to raise funds for the war effort. His son-in-law was serving in the Australian armed forces. After his arrest, he made numerous, but unsuccessful appeals for his release and for innocence to be recognized. For many years after his release, he sought to have his name cleared, but to no avail. When, some years after his passing, Liz had the opportunity to undertake thorough historical research as part of her education as a history teacher, she turned to the question, which had vexed her grandfather. It was my pleasure to be her academic supervisor for this thesis.

The particular issue investigated here relates to the important question of the rights of British subjects in Australia in this period. This can also be related to the rights and protections inherent in being an Australian citizen today. In the years after federation and before the creation of the category of Australian citizen in 1948 (Australian Citizenship Act), most Australians of British heritage enjoyed the status of British subject with the associated protections in relation to the power of the state over them.

Australian notions of the rule of law have often been seen as dating back to the Magna Carta of 1215 and subsequent legal developments which guaranteed the rights and freedom of the individual in the community and in relation to government. Such rights were assumed by the people of Australia. However there were exceptions. The Australian Federation of 1901 and the Australian Constitution were based upon the desire to maintain Australia as a white nation and to exclude those deemed to be non-white, including the South Sea Islanders who had built up the Queensland sugar industry, the Indian and Afghan hawkers who brought supplies to remote stations and isolated communities and the Chinese who joined the gold-rushes in Victoria and New South Wales. These, often long-standing Australian residents, were declared to be aliens. Indeed, some of these from British India and from the British colony of Hong Kong were in fact British subjects and should by rights have enjoyed all the privileges of being a British subject. They were denied these due to their 'race'.[i]

Another exception concerned Australians, whose family background was in a country with which Australia was at war. They were regarded with great suspicion in war-time. They were deemed to be white but they could be denied their rights as British subjects and of a fair trial. J.F.W. Schulz was impacted by the anti-German hysteria, which affected the wider Australian community in both the world wars, when the German state was an enemy of the Australian government and people.

During the First World War this had affected him adversely as the German language schools, where he had been a teacher were closed down in 1917. Thus he had to abandon his vocation and take up a new occupation as a manager and later owner of a printing business in Tanunda. 1936 was the centenary year of South Australia and those whose families had originally come from Germany celebrated their pioneers, like other South Australians. They were rightly proud of their achievements and celebrated the strength of the German language and social customs in their Australian home. They were Australian, but valued their cultural heritage. J.F.W. Schulz helped maintain the German language and at his print-shop produced publications in German for the Lutheran church of Australia.

The rise of the German Nazi party roused much attention around the world and some South Australians of German background were supportive of these developments. Just as in the current environment, governmental authorities and security forces found it hard to distinguish between those who wished to maintain some of their cultural heritage in Australia and those who supported the enemy cause.

The civil liberty issues and the challenge of an Australian population drawn from across the world with strong cultural ties to their homeland continue to cause problems for Australian citizens and their government. This thesis draws out these issues in the story of J.F.W. Schulz and his struggle for justice in the 1940s.

Margaret Allen
Professor Emerita Margaret Allen
University of Adelaide
November 2023.

i. Margaret Allen, 'I am a British subject': Indians in Australia claim rights, 1880-1940', *History Australia,* 15 (3) 2018, 499-518. Also K. Bagnall and P. Prince (eds) *Aliens and Subjects: Histories of Nationality, Law and Belonging in Australia and New Zealand,* ANU Press, 2023.

INTRODUCTION

This is a study of the experiences of my grandfather, Johann Friedrich Wilhelm Schulz, who was Australian born of German descent. His parents had emigrated from Silesia in 1881 and he grew up within a German-Australian environment. He spoke German fluently, wrote books in a Silesian dialect, taught in Lutheran Church schools prior to World War One, was a leading businessman in the Tanunda district, and prior to his internment during World War Two was the local endorsed A.L.P. candidate for the State elections.

In this study, I will show that he was wrongfully interned. All the evidence for his internment was circumstantial. In fact, he was condemned for maintaining his German heritage within the Australian society. It is interesting to note that now such behaviour is an approved part of our multicultural society. The wartime defence regulations undermined his basic legal rights and condemned him to three years imprisonment and one year of labour under direction of the State. Despite persistent efforts on his part he was never exonerated.

I have researched the issues surrounding his internment using family records, his personal diaries and letters, and Government records in the Australian Archives.

It is necessary to explore the history of the early and subsequent Lutheran settlers and their influence on the growth of South Australia to fully comprehend the impact these people had on the development of this State. They were a close-knit community in their various settlement areas and their reluctance to become totally absorbed into Anglo-Australian culture formed the seedbed of alienation. The internment issues are merely a harvest crop of these cultural differences.

For the families of those interned during World War Two it was a time of bewilderment and shame. The Lutheran Church, its ministers and school teachers, were under constant suspicion. In everyday conversations, the most innocent remarks were invariably misconstrued, and neighbour spied on neighbour.

The internment issue is still a sensitive one in South Australia. Many were wrongfully interned and were never given the chance to prove their innocence. This desire to clear his name prompted my grandfather to write the following thoughts some years after his release.

> *'I took the present as I found it and buried the past in my diary. It dates from December 13, 1940, to January 5, 1944, the period in which I lived in compulsory retirement. Amusing, interesting, exciting and heartbreaking incidents are recalled to memory, revealing evermore definitely how the powers that were had availed themselves of artistic mouldings of the unshapely clay of truth and sickly malarious forms of intrigue.*
>
> *I owe it to the many friends who stood loyally behind me, my family and my business, to publicly wash the pan of dirt, to carry the lies down the drain and to lay bare the few grains of eighteen carat gold that remain.*
>
> *When I look back over the months and review them in retrospect there are desert wastes from which the memory winces like some tired traveller faced with a dreary stretch of road. Even from the security of later rest and happiness I cannot contemplate them without a shudder.*
>
> *Magna Carta, we are informed, was sent to the United States for safe keeping late in 1939, but it still is the charter*

for British liberties, setting out that each person is to be held innocent until proven guilty.

My challenge is the production of proof calling for my internment.'

1

Germans in South Australia Before World War One

'Not Germans, not Englishmen: we want to be Australians', such were the words of Dr. Muecke in 1875. He and Basedow asserted that the German settlers loved the colonies more truly than the British who often regarded them merely as temporary locations in which they would acquire treasure with which to return home. They saw the Australian colonies as analogues of the American crucible, fusing diverse peoples into one.

> B. Walker. "German Language Press and People in South Australia, 1848 – 1900" Royal Australian Historical Society Journal, Vol. 58, part 2, 1972. p. 135

The colony of South Australia, as envisaged by a group of British gentlemen who called themselves The South Australian Association, was conceived in 1831. Negotiations were begun with the British Government to pass an Act defining the limits of the new colony and appointing Commissioners to execute the specifications of this

Act. The object of these men was to establish a new colony with its emphasis not in convictism, but in a combination of labour and capital. People who had money to pay for their own passage out to South Australia and who could purchase land on which to settle, would be encouraged to do so. The Association would then use this money to assist other immigrants to the colony to work the land and make it productive.[1] The Act was passed in August 1834 and one of a number of Commissioners appointed was George Fife Angas, a Christian philanthropist who, in an effort to prevent the scheme from failing, became one of the Directors of The South Australian Company. This company assisted in the buying and settlement of land in South Australia. Under this scheme, whole families were encouraged to emigrate, in fact, one clause of the Act stated that "no person having a husband or wife, or a child or children shall, by means of the emigration fund, obtain a passage to the Colony, unless the husband or wife, or the child or children of such poor person shall be conveyed thither."[2] Any person convicted of a crime was automatically rejected as an emigrant, and all persons arriving by ship from Western Australia, where convicts were accepted, had to show official clearance before being permitted to settle in the colony. It was also intended that British subjects were to be given preference as assisted emigrants.

While The South Australian Company was trying to find suitable emigrants to build up the small colony of South Australia, a group of German Lutherans in Prussia were undergoing severe restrictions in their form of worship due to the formation of the State Church of Prussia by Frederick William the Third, King of Prussia. This State Church was a union of Reformed and Lutheran Churches formed in 1817. A new liturgy was issued in 1822[3] which contained doctrines varying considerably from the faith and confessions of these Lutherans. Because of the pressure brought to bear on these

'Old Lutherans' who would not conform, a group at Klemzig in Brandenburg, Prussia, with Pastor August Ludwig Christian Kavel as their spiritual leader, decided to emigrate in order to continue worshipping according to their own doctrinal beliefs.[4] They had applied to the King for tolerance in his attitude toward their faith during October, 1835, stating their thoughts as follows:

> *'We feel constrained to emigrate rather than deny our faith. Thus we give proof that the Lutheran Church is not concerned with earthly goods, nor with power over men, nor with dissolution of the Union, but with liberty of conscience pure and simple.'*[5]

Kavel was sent to Hamburg during the early part of 1836 hoping to arrange the necessary details for emigration to America, but no-one was willing to provide finance. It was suggested that he contact a Mr. George Fife Angas in London who was looking for family groups to emigrate and establish the new colony of South Australia. Mr. Angas was looking for "honest, industrious and pious colonists",[6] and had written in his diary: "For the success of the colony I look only to God… If only I succeed in securing God-fearing people, God will bless that land."[7] His prayer was answered with the subsequent meeting in London between himself and Pastor Kavel.

Kavel's group had originally intended leaving Germany on June 8th, 1836, but the Government refused all applications for passports because they had not been applied for individually but as one group. Further applications to the King proved futile. Eventually Kavel appealed to the King stating that many members of the group were suffering hardship because they had sold all their belongings in readiness for the journey and were now dependent on the assistance of others, many of whom were in a similar situation. However, it was not until the end of 1837, after providing documents to the effect that they would be given the opportunity to support themselves in their new land, and that a minister of their faith would accompany them, that they were finally given permission to leave Germany.

The present city of Adelaide grew from a settlement founded by two shiploads of colonists who arrived during 1836-37. Approximately forty of these were Germans. On June 8th, 1838, the first of three groups of Lutherans, (approximately 250 people) embarked on their journey to a new home in South Australia. They boarded the river boats which took them along the River Oder to Frankfurt, then via the Friedrich Wilhelm Canal to Berlin. From there they travelled along the River Spree to Hamburg where they boarded the Prince George. The next stage of the journey to Adelaide was via Plymouth Harbour in England where Pastor Kavel joined them. He had spent the previous two years in England, working and learning the language. This first group arrived in South Australia on Sunday, November 20th, 1838.[8]

Here in South Australia they were promised the freedom of conscience denied them in Prussia because one of the founding principles on which South Australia was established was that there would be no State Church[9] as had occurred in Prussia, and all colonists would be free to choose their own method of worship.

Two other groups of Lutherans followed Pastor Kavel's group to settle in the new colony. 197 people on the 'Zebra' with Captain Hahn arrived on 29th December, 1838 and 130 people on the 'Catherina' arrived on January 25th, 1839. The total number of Lutherans in the colony at this time was 570, which amounted to 10% of the total population.[10](See Map 1 and Table 1.)

Between 1838-1900 many Germans emigrated to South Australia not because of religious difficulties but often because of glowing reports sent by relatives and friends about the opportunities for advancement in the colony. Spurred on by these reports and pressured by the failure of potato and cereal crops during the years 1836, 1842-3, and 1846-7, and the depressed state of industries such as the weaving industry of Hanover,[11] many Germans were prompted to try their fortunes elsewhere.

After 1848 other types of Germans saw Australia as a land of promise. These were a better educated and wealthier group of people interested in trade, politics and social interaction. Many of these were professional people who became absorbed more readily into the social life of the larger towns and who soon began to adopt a dual nationality. They did not retain their ethnic and language heritage exclusively, but spoke English and integrated the English customs with their German traditions. Table 1 shows the trend in migration to South Australia between the years 1861-1900. The greatest influx is shown during the years 1881-1890 with a total of 2,243 German immigrants. At the Census of 1871, 25% of the population were of English birth, 8% Irish, 4.5% Scottish, 4.5% German, 55% South Australian born and the remaining 3% from other British colonies.[12]

Pastor Kavel's group of Lutherans settled on 150 acres of land near the River Torrens which they rented from Mr. Angas for seven years. This settlement was named Klemzig after the village in which Pastor Kavel had previously ministered to his congregation. The second group settled on land near Mount Barker which belonged to a Mr. Dutton. They named this settlement 'Hahndorf' in recognition of the support and help their Captain Hahn had given them on the journey out. The third group formed a settlement at Glen Osmond near the foothills of Mount Lofty, but after a few years these people moved in with the other groups because there was not enough room to expand as the other groups had.[13]

In 1839 land was bought in the Barossa Valley from Mr. Angas. Pastor Kavel could see the need for the Klemzig group to eventually own their own land in an area which provided room for growth, particularly as many of the Glen Osmond group had joined them. But there was one other reason which proved to be a significant fact in the ability of this group to retain their ethnicity. Pastor Kavel had decided it was necessary to find suitable land away from the urban settler's influences and further inland, "where the members of the various congregations might come together to form one settlement, in which case the church life would benefit and the spiritual ministry be very much simplified."[14] Therefore, it would appear that in an effort to make his ministerial duties easier to execute by not having to travel such long distances, he unwittingly sowed the seeds for the instigation of closed communities of German-Australians.

Of the eighteen religious denominations recorded at the 1871 Census, German Lutherans comprised 8.30% of the population, preceded by Weslyan Methodists 14.59%, Roman Catholics 15.44%, and Church of England 27.39%.[15]

The Lutheran Church was most influential in the everyday life of these early settlers. From the years 1840 onwards there developed an idea that in order to keep the Lutheran faith intact all Lutherans living outside Germany must keep their German heritage alive: a heritage comprising language, customs and culture. For this reason those early settlers continued to live a way of life very similar to that in Germany. In fact, it "seemed as though a little piece of Silesia had suddenly taken wings and flown complete and undisturbed to a new land many thousands of miles away."[16] These people were of poor, uneducated stock who lived frugally and worked hard to repay their debt to Mr. Angas. They needed to speak very little English to sell their produce to the English speaking townspeople, and their other daily activities involved their fellow Germans, hence the lack of incentive to learn the English language. Slowly but surely this inability to communicate fortified the barriers already established through differences in religion and culture between the German and English speaking groups of the colony.

The German settlers believed their land was God-given and, as such, should be maintained and utilized to the best of their ability. It was an asset to be handed on to future generations and was proof of acceptance of their new country.

Those years of early settlement were filled with days of hard pioneering work. Buildings were erected from whatever happened to be at hand; they were virtually hewn from the surrounding scrub. The cleared timber was used for the framework, roof, door posts, window sills, and indoor furniture. The straw which had grown in their fields was used to thatch the roof and the clay from their land made the walls since brick or stone had to be bought with money, and money was scarce.

Francis Dutton, in South Australia and its Mines (1846), makes the following comment on the character of those early German settlers:

> '... the necessity of every farthing he spends, is seriously weighed, before he parts with it, you never see a German in a public house drinking spirits; he will come into the town many miles afoot, carrying, perhaps, a heavy load of vegetables, of what not, for the market; after he has sold his goods, he will take a lump of bread out of his pocket, brought with him from home, of his housewife's own baking, and his day's profit must have been very good to induce him to buy even a glass of ale to wash down his frugal dinner; more frequently it is a draught of spring water...'[17]

The majority of these German Lutherans were farmers, rural labourers or tradesmen, in fact 82% of those from Eastern Germany who were naturalised between 1848 and 1900 fitted into these categories.[18] Lutheran group settlements consisted almost entirely of farmers and thereby provided these new Australians with the potential as land owners to influence the social and cultural development of these new communities.

The Barossa Valley is in close proximity to Adelaide and these Lutheran farmers were able to provide fruit, vegetables, dairy produce, meat and small goods to the urban settlers (see Map 2). The geographical situation of the valley itself enclosed and protected its inhabitants from outside influences. It was a virtual fortress against assimilation and provided a barrier to change.

Until the year 1900 there seems to have been a tendency for immigrants from the eastern sections of Germany to settle in the areas established by the earlier arrivals from those same areas. Their religion and language formed a common bond and, I believe, enabled them to adjust more readily to their new environment (see Map 3).

These group settlements hindered intermarriage and enabled the religious and cultural aspects of their lives to continue without the changes which occurred to the Germans who interacted with English speaking groups in the larger towns. Marriage with persons of other cultural and religious beliefs was not encouraged by the Lutheran Church since it "represented a weakening both of Lutheran religious values and of the cohesiveness of the German migrant groups."[19] It would have proved a stumbling block to the continued use of German as the primary source of communication and instruction.

Although these immigrants intended to retain their ties with Germany, they showed no hesitation in accepting British citizenship. Between the years 1848 and 1900, almost one half of the Germans in South Australia (approximately 48%) applied for naturalisation within their first five years of residency. 15% applied within twelve months.[20] The remainder applied only after they had been in the country for ten years or more (See Table 2).[21] It has been suggested that the explanation for this time interval which applies after 1860 may be due in part to "an ever increasing sense of loyalty to the growth of a new German nation which reached its final goal in Europe with the defeat of France in 1871."[22] So it appears that many German-born Australians had no difficulty in accommodating a dual nationality, and naturalisation was seen as the final step toward acceptance of this new home.

The first three groups of Lutheran settlers had come halfway round the world to realize their dream of religious freedom, and with this now a reality, had benefitted in their need to create a new society based on their traditional virtues of industry and thrift. If their land was, as they regarded it, "a Divine trust for the future"[23] then it is possible to appreciate that the continuing generations would tend to be under pressure to retain their family ties, and remain either on or near the homestead. The desire to keep their communities entirely German in character brought with it the very basic sense of security these settlers needed. Language and faith were entwined. As the editor of Auricht's Almanac records in 1927:

> 'As we are to honour our parents we cannot but feel esteem for the nation from which we sprang. ... the fact that Germany is the home of the Reformation, makes this country and its people near and dear to us. All that is precious to us in our own spiritual lives and in the life of our church, came from German sources.'[24]

Many believed that if they lost their language in the transition toward assimilation into the Australian way of life, then they would also lose their history. This loss would include the German Bible, catechism, the spiritual and other literature of their homeland, and most importantly, the traditions and customs of their forebears.

First generation Australians born of German parentage knew no other language until they reached the age when contact with the outside world necessitated their learning English, either for the purposes of education or employment. The Lutheran Church insisted on educating the young within their own schools and maintained that religious instruction should form the central point of the child's education. The Church believed that the influences and ideals conveyed to these children should come from Christian teachers whose faith was the same as that of the parents. In these schools the education of first and second generation Australians was conducted in German, thereby maintaining cultural ties with Germany.

Historically, education has been one of the major functions of the Church, although during the 1850s there were moves to start separate State and Church education based on the concept of public responsibility for education. Education Acts during the period 1851-1870 expanded education, making it more widely available and accepting the principle that the government must be more financially responsible.

The Act of 1852 set the secular base for education in South Australia based on common Christianity, and free, secular, and compulsory education was introduced with the Act of 1875. Therefore, education was seen as a public, social responsibility whereby all children were to have available to them a school system run by the State, free of charge, and paid for by all citizens.

Much of the debate leading up to the passage of the Education Act of 1875 revolved around the issue of the use of the Bible in schools. It was suggested that the Bible was a most objectionable book to be allowed into the hands of children without explanation and that if there was explanation then it would be considered as doctrinal.

Many Germans feared that this would be a vehicle for dissolving Deutschtum.[25] They saw these reforms as hindering the progress of German culture and consciousness. They also believed that eventually they would lose their educational control to the State schools because of the necessity for education in the English language.

Price suggests that:

> 'in seeking a solution for genuine religious needs and problems the church tended to find it in a pan-Germanic[26] direction rather than any other... education of the young people was framed in a definite German background... when the young people were demanding more instruction in English, the Church intensified its programme for educating its following in the ways of Deutschtum.'[27]

I disagree with Price's view regarding his statement that the Church intensified its programme. It should be seen as a continuation of an existing policy rather than an intensification of any programme. For these Lutherans it was important that their children received a Christian education and they stated:

> 'We maintain our own schools in order that our children, besides being instructed in all the secular subjects comprised in the State school course, may also receive daily instruction in religion, and that their entire education, also the secular part, may be in the hands of earnest Christian teachers.'[28]

Religion and education in the German language were not the only means of communication these people had with their German heritage. Contact with Germany was certainly maintained through the guiding control of the Lutheran Church, but also by correspondence with relatives and friends in the homeland. Information on German affairs, both political and otherwise, was also provided by the South Australian German language Press. This began with the publication of the Sued-Australische Zeitung in 1861, a newspaper which contained foreign and local political news and feature articles on agricultural subjects. The political attitude of the Press toward Germany at that time could be regarded as pan-Germanic. Information was given about the various independent States of Germany with an impartial but conservative viewpoint. As Derek van Abbe states: "The foreign articles were thorough and well documented and, it might be remarked, by no means restricted to European politics."[29]

In March, 1863, another German-language paper, the Tanunda Deutsche Zeitung, began publication. In 1870 this was changed to the Australische Deutsche Zeitung, and in 1875 this newspaper and the Sued-Australische Zeitung amalgamated to become the Australische Zeitung, which called itself "the only German newspaper in all the Australias".[30]

These newspapers provided information not only of a political nature but also of interest to the farming communities. The interests of the women were not catered for since the owner and editor, Friedrich Basedow, "a believer in 'Kueche, Kirche, Kinder' (kitchen, Church, children) for women-kind evidently expected that the Hausfrau (housewife) would not read the main paper but only the entertainment supplement.[31]

The declared aims of the German-language Press were partly those common to the liberal Press as a whole, such as the promotion of truth, morality, progress and patriotism, and partly those specially relating to Deutschum - promoting pride in the German nation, fostering the German language and culture, maintaining links with the fatherland and also influencing colonial life in a German way.[32]

The Lutheran Church began publication of its first newspaper, the Kirchen und Missions Zeitung fuer Deutsch-Australische Gemein in 1862 at Tanunda.[33] It was the semi-official paper of the Evangelical Lutheran Immanuel Synod in Australia, which later became known as the U.E.L.C.A. Synod. In January, 1874, Der Lutherische Kirchenbote fuer Australien was published in Adelaide by the other main branch of the Lutheran Church, the E.L.C.A. Synod.[34] These two papers, as well as the secular German press and a number of magazine type publications, provided the German reading population with religious, cultural and political information for almost sixty years.

By the eve of World War One, German-Australian communities were well established in South Australia. The members of these communities were generally well respected and, on the whole, considered to be industrious, frugal, God-fearing people. They were a distinct group in that their traditions had not changed from those of the first settlers. Their life revolved around their faith. Each Saturday evening at sunset church bells would be rung as a reminder for the faithful to discharge their earthly toil for the week, and to prepare themselves for worship and the Lord's work on the following day. This tradition still continues in many of the towns to this day.

***

1. Quoted by D. Whitelock, Adelaide 1836—1976. History of Difference, p. 67.
2. W.D. Borrie, Italians and Germans in Australia, p. 194.

3. C.A. Price, "German Settlers in South Australia, 1838—1900" Historical Studies Australia and New Zealand Journal, vol. 7, No. 28, May 1957, p. 450.
4. Refer to H. Homburg in South Australian Lutherans and Wartime Rumours, p. 58. He states that "official records show that the Lutheran leader and all his flock became naturalized Australians promptly on Arrival."
5. W.D. Borrie, Italians and Germans in Australia, p. 158.
6. Ibid, p. 186.
7. C.A. Price, German Settlers in South Australia, 1838—1900" Historical Studies Australia and New Zealand Journal, vol. 7, No. 28, May 1957. p.447.
8. Auricht's Almanac, 1927, p. 64.
9. "Deutschtum" — German culture, customs, and language.
10. "Pan-Germanic" — completely German
11. C.A. Price, German Settlers in South Australia, p. 21.
12. The Lutheran Church in Australia and its Schools, p. 14.
13. D. Van Abbe, "The Interests of the South Australian German Language Press in the Nineteenth Century", Historical Studies Australia and -New - Zealand Journal, Vol. 8, No. 31, Nov. 1958, p. 319.
14. R. B Walker, "German Language Press and People in South Australia, 1848-1900", Royal Australian Historical Society Journal, Vol. 58, part 2, 1972, p. 125.
15. Ibid, p. 129.
16. Ibid, p. 126.
17. M. Gilson and J. Zubrzycky, The Foreign Language Press in Australia. 1848-1964, p. 11.
18. Ibid, p. 12.
19. W. Harcus, South Australia, p .4.
20. Ibid, p. 5.

21. A. Grenfell Price, Founders and Pioneers of South Australia, p. 197.
22. Refer to I. Harmstorf in The Germans in Australia, p. 12. He states that emigration had been allowed under the 1555 Treaty of Augsburg.
23. Th. Hebart, The United Evangelical Lutheran Church in Australia, p .26.
24. Ibid, P.27.
25. Ibid, P. 27.
26. Ibid, pp. 32-33.
27. W. Harcus, South Australia, p. 6.
28. Th. Hebart, The United Evanaelical Lutheran Church in Australia, pp. 34-35.
29. C.A. Price, " German Settlers in South Australia, 1838—1900" Historical Studies Australia and New Zealand Journal, vol. 7, No. 28, May 1975, p. 441.
30. W. Harcus, South Australia, p. 224.
31. Th. Hebart, The United Evangelical Lutheran Church in Australia, pp. 37-40.
32. Ibid, p. 42.
33. W Harcus, South Australia, p. 229.
34. C.A. Price, German Settlers in South Australia, p. 13.

Map 1

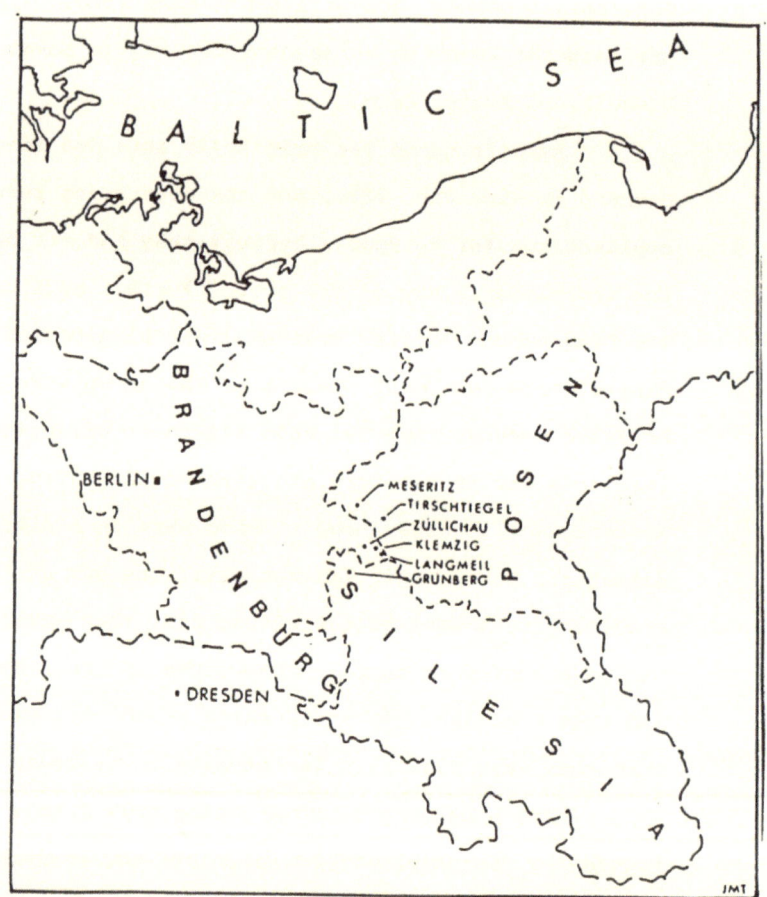

Central Prussia in 1844, showing villages in the areas from which the 'Old Lutherans' emigrated to South Australia with Pastors Kavel and Fritzsche (From Black's General Atlas (Edinburgh, 1844)).

Map 2

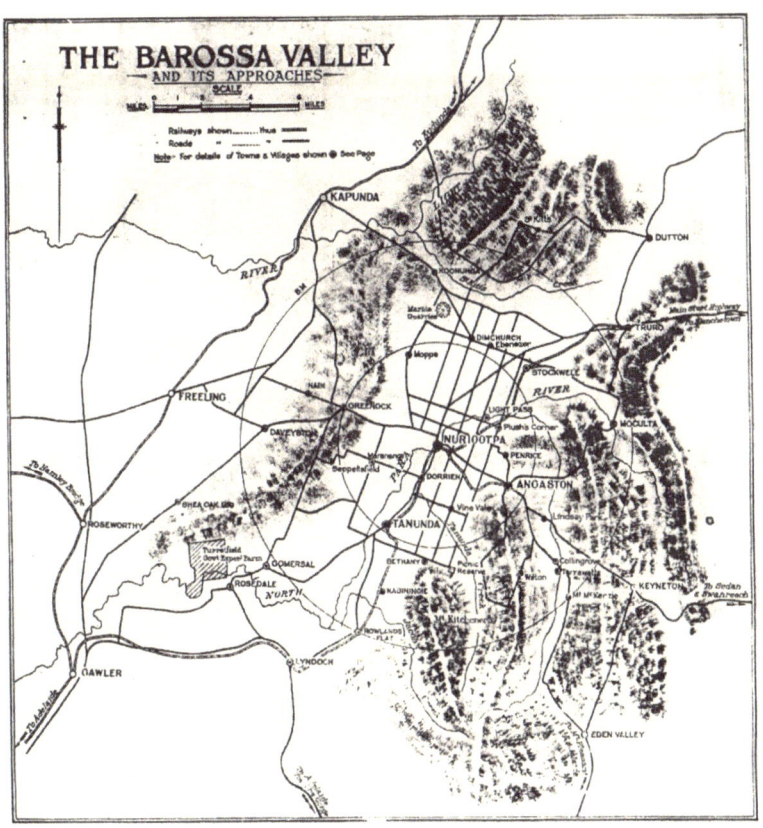

Table 1

Table I
GERMAN IMMIGRATION TO SOUTH AUSTRALIA
1861–1900

	Males	Females	Children	Total
1861–1870	560	359	331	1,250
1871–1880	793	411	503	1,707
1881–1890	1,210	547	486	2,243
1891–1900	490	192	86	768
1861–1900	3,053	1,509	1,406	5,968

Table 2
APPLICATIONS FOR NATURALIZATION BY GERMANS, SOUTH AUSTRALIA, 1848–1900

	Age at Naturalization	Number of Cases Examined	Interval in Years between Arrival and Naturalization. Percentage Distribution				
			0–1	1–4	5–9	10 and over	Total
Naturalized before 1860	Under 30	167	9·58	61·68	19·76	8·98	100·00
	30–39	160	13·75	67·50	16·88	1·87	100·00
	40–49	93	8·60	64·52	23·66	3·22	100·00
	50 and over	38	10·53	44·74	39·47	5·26	100·00
	Total	458	10·92	62·88	21·18	5·02	100·00
Naturalized after 1860	Under 30	243	37·86	30·04	13·99	18·11	100·00
	30–39	240	14·17	17·08	17·92	50·83	100·00
	40–49	178	5·62	7·30	8·43	78·65	100·00
	50 and over	154	1·30	1·95	5·84	90·91	100·00
	Total	815	16·93	15·95	12·39	54·73	100·00
Total	Under 30	410	26·34	42·93	16·34	14·39	100·00
	30–39	400	14·00	37·25	17·50	31·25	100·00
	40–49	271	6·64	26·94	13·65	52·77	100·00
	50 and over	192	3·12	10·42	12·50	73·96	100·00
	Total	1,273	14·77	32·84	15·55	36·84	100·00

Map 3

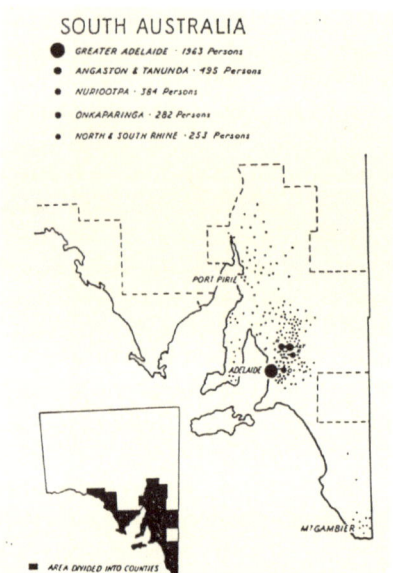

Distribution of persons of German birthplace in South Australia at the census of 1891.
1 dot = 25 persons Circles to scale.

Plotted by corporations and district councils. Circles refer to district councils (except 'Greater Adelaide' circle, which refers to several corporations).

2

J.F.W. Schulz and Family Before World War Two

"I said to the man who stood at the gate of the year; 'Give me a light that I may tread safely into the unknown,' and he replied: Go out into the darkness and put your hand into the hand of God. That shall be to you better than light and safer than a known way."
    M. Louise Haskins

One of the many families which made the long journey from Germany to South Australia during the nineteenth century was Johann Gottfried Schulz, his wife Johanne Maria Elizabeth and three children, Pauline, Paul and Bertha, aged nine, four and one years respectively. They left the small village of Thiemendorf in the district of Crossen on the River Oder in Silesia, to emigrate to South Australia in June 1881. Gottfried was thirty seven and Maria thirty two years of age.

    They had decided to settle in the area between Point Pass and Robertstown because an uncle of Gottfried's, a Schild who had emigrated in 1866, had written to the family in Germany begging them to emigrate because of the opportunities for a better standard of living in South Australia. The poor sandy soil around the village had made farming difficult and a succession of poor harvests had left the villagers in bad circumstances.

Gottfried had a good position with the Railways in Raednitz, a town near Thiemendorf, and many of the villagers wondered why he had decided to leave. The success which Schild had experienced must have been the deciding factor since it seems certain that without his help Gottfried would never have left Thiemendorf.

Gottfried's younger brother, Johann Gottlob, drove the family together with a cousin Wilhelm Mueller, in horse and cart to Raednitz across the River Oder where they transferred to the train which took them to Hamburg. Here they embarked on a ship for England. The two mothers of the travellers wept on their knees as their sons left the village. Schulz and Mueller were also very upset and seemed sad at having to leave home. But Gottfried's mother said, in the dialect of that area: "Nu husst du daer's ma vurgenumm, nu musst de uch giehn." (You have promised to go, so now you must go.)[1]

In England the Schulz family and Mueller embarked on the Stirlingshire and left Plymouth harbour on July 8th, 1881 arriving at Port Adelaide on September 21st, 1881. The cost of the passage for the two adults was four pounds each, three pounds each for the two elder children and free passage for Bertha[2] who, according to a daughter of hers, learnt to walk on the voyage out.

Little is known of the Schulz family during their first few years in South Australia. They built a small home on farming land between Point Pass and Robertstown where Gottfried worked the land. He took on labouring jobs in the nearby towns to help their finances. They continued their German traditions, worshipping each Sunday in the Lutheran Church at Point Pass.

Johann Friedrich Wilhelm Schulz, the subject of this study, was the first child born in the family home in South Australia. He was the second son and was born on 19th March, 1883. On 26th August, 1883, he was baptized at Immanuel Lutheran Church, Point Pass by Pastor Johannes M. Stolz. Thus he was the Australian born child of a recently arrived immigrant German family. He was raised in a strong German-Australian community and received his primary education at Point Pass school under the guidance of teacher Krichauff, with lesson instruction in German and English. His secondary education consisted almost entirely of lesson instruction in the English language. Immanuel College, the secondary school he attended, was founded at Point Pass in 1895 by Pastor Leidig. He was J. F.W. Schulz's pastor at this time, when his primary school days were at an end, and it is not surprising to find that Schulz was among the first nine pupils of the College.

> 'On the 5th September, 1894, Pastor Leidig of Point Pass boldly announced to Synod in session at Light's Pass his intention of founding a training institution for providing the necessary instruction for the confirmees in his outback congregations, for training teachers for Lutheran day schools, for upholding the language and culture of the fathers, and for general purposes.'[3]

Under Pastor Leidig, Schulz continued his studies at the College with the calling of Lutheran Day School teacher as his aim and goal. The following excerpt from a charming speech he gave at an Immanuel College Old Scholars Reunion in 1946, will give some idea of what this chance to further his education meant to him.

> 'I remember well the day soon after my Confirmation when my father announced that Pastor Leidig had asked him that I be permitted to enter his class at Point Pass with a view to becoming a private school teacher. Father had told the pastor that he

had been looking forward to receiving help from me; helping to work and earn money to keep our very humble home going. To all protestations Pastor Leidig had answered that he was asking for nothing other than that I be willing to continue study and that my clothing be found.

And so I entered Immanuel College as one of the first batch of students and for three long years I was boarded, taught and had washing done — later to sign an undertaking to pay thirty pounds in three annual instalments of ten pounds.

I commenced in 1897. There was at that time only the oblong first building, built by Mr. G. Dahlitz of Robertstown, my father acting as mason's labourer. The room nearest to the road was our study and classroom when Pastor Leidig himself taught, and for the subjects taught by Mr. Krichauff we went to the school after Mr. Krichauff had dismissed his day scholars.

Tante (Aunty) Krause was our "Hausmutter" (Housemother). Our meals were served in the pastor's kitchen, the untiring Frau Pastor with the assistance of Miss Agnes Krichauff (later Mrs. F. Jacob) attending to the preparation of the meals. Daily devotions, morning and evening after meals, were conducted in the room adjoining the pastor's study, Friedrich Jacob and Hermann Vogel sang invariably playing the harmonium.

Pastor Leidig with his far-flung parish: Point Pass, Robertstown, Baldina, Peep Hill, Geranium Plain, etc. and, as President of Immanuel Synod, had realized how necessary it was to have Gemeindeschullehrer (Parish school teachers), and almost the entire class at my time was being trained for that calling. When we realized that Pastor Leidig created this Preparatory School of his own initiative, that it was a private undertaking, placing on the shoulders of one man all the numerous and varied responsibilities, we shall the better be able to evaluate *how physically strong in body, mentally alert, and spiritually strong in faith the founder of Immanuel College, Pastor Leidig, must have been.*

In the teaching of subjects such as Algebra and Geometry in English, he had to grapple with the language, as President of Synod it devolved upon him to state and solve problems of his Church, and as editor of the Kirchen Zeitung, besides the usual work accumulating in the editorial office, he had to attend to inter-synodical controversies.

During my stay at the school, Mr. Both commenced erecting the larger building. Occasionally the supply of sand and stones threatened to run out, but after the pastor announced this fact at the conclusion of the usual announcements, members of the congregation soon had the necessary building material on hand again. While the carters of sand or stone were partaking of refreshments it devolved upon the students to unload the wagons. I remember breaking the glass of my pocket watch while unloading stones on one occasion. This evidence is not being tendered as an indication of hard work on my part but rather of my carelessness for wearing the watch at this work. Yes, I carried a watch and chain. Possibly a chain more than a watch, for I remember an occasion when the watch refused to continue giving tick. It required all the patience and perseverance of Fritz Jacob to get the numerous wheels back into position, also those which were over at the first attempt, until finally it dutifully carried on at the end of a chain.

Our one and only recreation on the grounds was an occasional game of croquet - a lady's game, the only female member of our class, Miss Geyer, being precluded from joining in the game.

Motor cars were not in evidence in those days. The horse and trap was our principal's means of locomotion when duty called him, in his far-flung parish. At one stage Pastor Leidig had three horses. A newly recruited, well broken-in pair of young piebalds soon broke out in unheard of antics when a trip was about to commence, that the driver after having safely negotiated the gate to the road had perforce to head southwards when the journey lay to the north! Occasionally we, the students, had to attend to the harnessing and unharnessing, had to remove the pale, attach the shafts and then commission the faithful chestnut Tyro, who was well past the voting stage on life's way, to do the job single-footed!

In due course a class was ready to proceed to Adelaide to sit at the first University Exam, the Preliminary. There were four in the party. It was my first train journey and my first visit to the city. Pastor Leidig had made arrangements for our reception at Mrs. Gleiber's Boarding House immediately opposite the Adelaide Railway Station. Both our teachers had made us take along the text books for the various subjects we were to be examined in.

The examination took place in the Adelaide Town Hall. Candidates were allotted little tables marked in alphabetical order. I found mine immediately behind the big organ which barred my view through the spacious hall where I might have been enabled to see one or the other of my comrades. I felt very lonely-as a matter of fact we all did. We envied the large parties of candidates who arrived at the Town Hall door from the Adelaide Colleges wearing distinctive blazers and badges. We stood reverently by until the doors opened and ushers, upon presentation of our cards, directed us to our seats. I remember the title of the composition we were asked to write at the examination:

Country Life versus Town Life. Well, I had lived in the country all my life and town life was crowding in on us right now. I believe we all did well in our examination on this subject, and I believe we all obtained a pass at this our first examination.

About Christmas 1900 it became fairly certain that I was to take charge of the Light's Pass School. Playing the church organ was an auxiliary duty of the teacher. The playing of any musical instrument was a weakness with me which I never assisted to grow into strength, and though Pastor Leidig had a small harmonium sent to my parents' home during the Christmas of 1900 that I might perfect myself in this art, I am afraid that I gave a poor showing when called to Light's Pass in a try-out. Fortunately the old Light's Pass Church organ suffered from an asthmatic wheeze at that time and when the two of us mutilated famous composers I have reason to believe that the organ was debited with much of the disharmony.[4]

Schulz's first teaching assignment was in the Barossa Valley at Light's Pass Lutheran School from 1901-1903. During 1903 he transferred to Queensland where he was appointed teacher of the Bethania Parish. He taught for four days per week at Bethania, on Fridays he taught at Beenleigh, and on Saturdays at Eagleby. At the latter place, his services were irregular as he was not keen on conducting school on a Saturday, much to the delight of the pupils.

In 1906 he travelled south to marry Ernstine Caroline Kruschel at Light's Pass on the 26th April. The service was conducted by Dr. John J. Stolz. The couple returned to Queensland and Schulz continued to serve the Church as teacher at Bethania and later at Laidley. In 1911 he accepted a call to teach at the Tanunda Lutheran Day School until the school was closed by the Government as a wartime measure in 1917.[5]

On the 13th June, 1916, the Inspector of Schools, Mr. T. W. Cole, made the following report after his annual inspection of the Tanunda Lutheran School. This report tells us something of the schools in which Schulz worked and also indicates the concern of the State authorities that the children learn English.

> 'I paid a short visit to this school on the morning of Friday, June 9th. There were present 61 children out of 64 on the Roll. The Head Teacher, Mr. J. F.W. Schulz, had helping him a lady-assistant.
>
> The children were well behaved and attentive in their lessons. Each child in answering the Roll call was required to repeat one line of the multiplication table. The children in the upper grades can speak English correctly and with ease.
>
> The Head Teacher says that outside of their homes they use the English language more frequently than their own. I talked to them for a short time, and heard them sing two or three songs, of which the National Anthem was one.
>
> I advised the Head Teacher to rewrite his Time-Table and to make it show clearly that the required four hours were devoted to the teaching of English. At present it does represent exactly what is being done.
>
> An application has been made for Mr. Schulz to be appointed teacher of Shorthand and Bookkeeping to the Continuation Classes. He is said to be a fine man by some English people to whom I spoke of him.'[6]

It is interesting to note that the Inspector felt it necessary to confirm the good character of Schulz by discussing him with 'English' people.

The war hysteria towards German-born Australians or those of German descent directly affected Schulz in his capacity as school teacher. During November, 1916, a Lutheran school teacher in the Barossa Valley had been accused in Parliament of disloyalty to the British flag by Mr. MacGillivray M.P. Schulz felt very strongly about this and wrote a personal appeal to Mr. MacGillivray during January, 1917, asking for an interview in order to settle the flag incident. Schulz felt that the name of the guilty person should have been made public in order to clear the names of innocent teachers. Letters to the editors of The Advertiser and The Register followed when he received no reply from Mr. MacGillivray, and he also wrote to the Commandant at the Military Headquarters in Keswick asking that an official investigation be instigated.[7]

Fear of the unknown, in this case the unknown being the German language and culture, including the Lutheran religion, created a gulf which the war hysteria widened out of all proportion. Various newspaper articles and letters only added fuel to the fire and Schulz, with his inherent cultural and religious attitude, not to mention his deep conviction regarding the freedom of the individual, fell victim to the petty bickerings and made what I suspect was his first mistake; that is, in writing his letter to the Military Authorities he made them aware of his attitude and possibly they in turn filed him as a suspected German sympathiser.

Schulz was actively involved in various local patriotic organisations during World War One, including the Tanunda Recruiting Committee, Belgian Relief Fund, South Australian Soldier's Fund, and the Local Repatriation Committee. In 1921, after having worked for various local businesses following the closure of Lutheran schools in 1917, he left South Australia to work in New Guinea for the Lutheran Mission. Prior to his departure he received a letter from Mr. C.A. Pollitt, who had been Chairman of the local patriotic organisations, in which thanks were extended for his pro-British attitude during the First World War. Pollitt considered that because Schulz was of German descent, the good work he had performed in the service of the Empire during the war had left a great impression of loyalty in his mind.[8]

Schulz spent eighteen months as storekeeper at the Lutheran Mission in Fischhafen before returning to his wife and family, who had stayed with relatives in Light's Pass and Mount Gambier during his absence, and together with them settled in Tanunda.

He was actively interested in politics. In 1920 he was appointed as one of the organisers of the Liberal Union prior to the 1921 elections. In 1925 he stood for election as one of the Liberal candidates to contest Barossa in the ensuing State elections.[9]

During 1926 Schulz began work at Auricht's Printing Office in the capacity of journalist and manager, learning various phases of the printing trade until finally in 1945 he took over the business. During this time his son Bert, who was born at Tanunda in 1913, had completed his education at Immanuel College, North Adelaide, and entered the printing trade as an apprentice at Auricht's Printing Office.

During the latter part of the 1920s, Schulz had begun writing articles and booklets in a Silesian dialect using the pen-name of August von der Flatt. He chose this name because many of the German descendants in the Barossa Valley and Murray Flat areas were especially fond of speaking their own South Australian version of the original Silesian dialect. In one letter to the editor of the Queensland Herald, using this pen-name, he commented on attitudes toward persons of German descent during the First World War.

> '...at that time everything that smelt German was to blame for the war. In Queensland, for example, the place called

Bethania was left with the same name; here in South Australia they quickly changed Bethanien into Bethany, Lobethal became Tweedvale, Hahndorf became Ambleside... Besides this, German was no longer allowed to be taught or learnt. German lessons had to stop. And now suddenly we are again 'jolly good fellows'... The thing that makes me somewhat annoyed at all this backscratching of the Germans ... is that there is an election in the offing and even people with German names have votes.'[10]

All of this had affected Schulz personally and he was understandably annoyed. His school had been closed and the career for which he had trained had been taken from him. In the role of journalist he used the vehicle of the written word to air his views. Unfortunately, once written and published, the meaning was all too often misconstrued, particularly in the post-World War One and pre-World War Two years.

Schulz's association with Dr. Johannes Becker began at a time when it could be reasonably assumed that Germany and Great Britain were reaching an understanding. Soon after Becker's arrival in Tanunda from Germany, during 1927, he became the Schulz family's medical adviser. Because of his interest in world politics, Becker occasionally gave Schulz German papers to read. On one occasion an argument ensued between the two men over Hitler's action regarding his order to shoot a number of his associates. Schulz's impression of Becker on issues other than medical is neatly summed up in this statement:

'In conversation with Becker you soon learned that there was only one side to any argument, and that was always Becker's side.'[11]

In 1934 Schulz's son, Bert, won the S.R. Delmont Medal and Scholarship for most brilliant and industrious student in his printing apprenticeship course. He gained a First Class pass in Composing, including best knowledge of English and Arithmetic. In order to gain experience in specialized printing, Schulz decided to send Bert to Germany where he would have the chance to work and observe detailed colour printing techniques. Through the assistance of Becker, who arranged for Bert to make contact with the Organisation of Germans Abroad, an organisation centred in Berlin, position was found with the printing firm Ullsteinhaus in Berlin.

Bert's stay in Germany coincided with the Centenary celebrations of the first settlers in South Australia. Many Australian born members of German families were eager to make contact with relatives still living in Germany during this time of remembrance and celebration, and people intending to travel to Germany on holidays were urged to visit the various areas from which the Lutheran pioneers had come. They were also urged to observe and comment on Hitler's new Germany and many of the comments they made to family in Australia found their way into the local newspapers.

1936 was also the year of the Olympic Games in Berlin, so news from Germany was of interest, not only in a political and historical sense to those of German origin, but also to those Australians who had no family ties with the country. Bert was authorised by Mr. E.W. Parish to act as one of the representatives of The Advertiser at the Olympic Games and was commissioned to write special articles of current interest for the newspaper.[12] Other articles he wrote were on the personality and power of Hitler as observed through the responses of the German people. Bert's comments on Hitler's election speeches, which began with the calling together of the Reichstag in Berlin on 7th March, 1936, give a vivid description of the attitude of the majority of Germans who believed in Hitler and were prepared to follow him. In one of the articles he states:

> 'The week before election day, March 29, was a succession of speeches. People might ask: "Why all this fuss; why all these appeals? Does Herr Hitler fear that the faith of the people is waning?" Not at all; the Fuhrer knows that these appeals are not necessary to retain his leadership. But he wishes to show the world that not one man made the memorable move of March 7th. Not one man, but a united Germany wants freedom, peace and equal rights.'[13]

The attitude of the people impressed Bert, and in many of his letters to family and friends in Australia he commented on their willingness to forgo luxuries for the good of the German nation; thoughts which many new Australians of German origin may have related to within the concept of doing without in order to establish their own new life in Australia.

Initially Bert was in awe of the response of so many Germans to the Hitler regime; a mass hysteria of political fervour which he had never experienced in his own country. Later he stated: "The more one hears Hitler speak, the more does one realize what a force this man is."[14] He considered that perhaps there was more to Hitler and his aims than people were initially aware of.

In order to write for the South Australian papers about the Olympic Games in Berlin, Bert visited Prince zu Schaumburg-Lippe at the propaganda Ministerium and was presented with a number of photographs of the Olympic Village and Stadium. This meeting was arranged through the Auslandsorganisation and Bert noted in his diary: "It seems as though the Auslandsorganisation had told him of me. The prince is very influential, it seems he takes his orders from Dr. Goebbels.[15] Bert was obviously unaware of the fact that he was a pawn in the game of German propaganda. The Auslandsorganisation would have been only too glad to give him information to send to Australia which would enhance the overseas view of the 'New Germany'.

Although J. F.W. Schulz's ties with Germany were limited, the letter which Bert wrote to him on 12th April, 1936, from the Schulz home at Thiemendorf must have moved him intensely. His letter begins in this way:

> *'This is perhaps the most important letter I have written during my stay in Germany so far. I am spending the Easter holidays in Thiemendorf where, in 1832, my great-grandfather was born - where in 1853 my great-grandfather was married. This morning I went to church in the ancient place of worship where in 1853 your father was christened. Yesterday I was in the room where his father spent his last days. I know what it would mean for you to see these places, and, by the same token, you will know how I appreciate what you have done for me... I only wish you had been able to walk with me along the narrow, sandy roadways and into the 'Hof'* (courtyard) *where your father's cradle stood. The little two-roomed house stands just as it did two centuries ago. When I went inside, there was an old lady baking 'Deutscher Kuchen' just as my great-great grandmother did years and years ago. Everything was just as it had been throughout the generations.'*[16]

Details of the Schulz family's departure from the village in 1881, information of other relatives, and aspects of village life and customs in 1936 filled the remaining pages of the letter. It was a link with the past for Schulz; similar traditions and beliefs, but in an unknown setting. His only other links with Germany were through the printing trade; books and pamphlets which were ordered for the Lutheran Church directly from Germany, and his involvement with the German Historical Society of South Australia of which he was a member.

Schulz's interest in politics was not confined to discussions with Dr. Becker. After many years as a Liberal party member, Schulz had withdrawn his affiliation with them during March, 1940, and applied for registration as a member of the Australian Labor Party[17] with a view to endorsement as a candidate for the 1941 State Elections. He considered that if there was to be a war, then it was the Labor Party who would support the Australian people through whatever crises occurred. He believed that Labor would be able effectively to control those paralysing forces which were the cause of so much unrest and suffering.[18]

***

1. From a letter written by Bert Schulz on a visit to Germany during 1936—37. In possession of the author.
2. Mortlock Library, Shipping Register for 1881.
3. Jubilee of Immanuel College, 1895—1945, p. 3.
4. Original manuscript in author's possession.
5. AA: D1915 File 1166, Lutheran Schools. Proposal to re-open.
6. Original manuscript in author's possession.
7. Copy of letter in author's possession.
8. AA: SS827, J. F. W. Schulz.
9. Copy of voting circular in author's possession.
10. SS827, J. F.W. Schulz.
11. Original manuscript in author's possession.
12. Memo from News Editor, May 21, 1936, in author's possession.
13. Copy of original article in author's possession.
14. Bert Schulz, Diary entry 27—3-1936.

15. Bert Schulz, Diary entry 20—5-1936.
16. Original letter in author's possession.
17. Original letter in author's possession.
18. Original manuscript in author's possession.

Illustration 2

Illustration 3

Illustration 4

Illustration 5

3

South Australia: Germans Between the Wars

"Enter the dream-house, brothers and sisters, leaving
Your debts asleep, your history at the door..."
C. Day Lewis: "Newsreel"

Prior to World War One, the German settlers were able to embrace a dual nationality, with their interest in maintaining the way of life and traditions of their German culture, combined with the necessary adaptations which the British expected. They did not think of Britain's war with Germany as any concern of theirs since they spoke of themselves as Australians. "Thus World War One in 1914 came as a traumatic shock to South Australia's Germans. It seemed to matter little to the government of the day whether people who spoke German were born in Germany or Australia."[1]

German nationals who, for one reason or another, had not become naturalised Australians were under suspicion as German sympathisers and interned. German communities as a whole were harassed. Newspaper headlines such as: "Arrogant Germans Still Hostile To The Empire. Best Lands Held By Germans-Why Not

Transfer Them To Diggers?"[2] provide some indication of the hatred felt toward those of German origin following the cessation of hostilities. But one of the most deeply felt accusations of guilt was the changing of sixty nine German place names by the South Australian Government in January, 1918. These were changed to English or Aboriginal names and "the history of nearly ten percent of the settlers of the colony was wiped out at a stroke; part of the heritage of every South Australian was lost in a moment of jingoistic passion."[3]

This public opinion had begun to harden gradually against those of German descent, particularly those in the group settlements. This first became noticeable during the late 1800s and early 1900s when international rivalry between the British Empire and the new German Empire began to increase. During November, 1919, a Royal Commission was held at Loxton, a town on the River Murray and one of a number of Lutheran group settlements, "to decide whether the district acknowledges its allegiance to the British Empire or not".[4] The Sunday Times in Sydney on 23rd November, advertised the incident in the following manner: "Loxton A Hotbed Of Hun Intrigue. Bitter Anti—British Feeling In South Australian Town. Repeated Attempts To Murder Constable. Royal Commission Investigating Whole Position."[5] Loxton, with many other towns which had been established by the early German settlers, had come under suspicion during the early months of the 1914-18 War because few of its young men of German descent had volunteered for active service. A number of people had been interned because of their "Hunnish sympathies"[6], and though Press censorship did not allow for publication of the facts, rumours spread about breaches of loyalty and pro-German sentiment. It was not until the lifting of this newspaper ban that various aspects of the so-called 'anti-British feeling' emerged. One paper, The Mail, "accused Loxton of such flagrant breaches of loyalty as a goose-step parade through the main street in 1914, an attempt by an alleged German or pro-German individual upon a policeman's life, the toasting of the Hun 'victory' when the Lusitania was torpedoed, and so on."[7]

Other information which did not appear in the Press includes an incident which clearly shows the pressure brought to bear on those who were 'different'. There was a local baker who had a German name. A number of residents of British extraction to whom he supplied bread continually refused to pay. They told the baker that since he was only a German, he didn't need to be paid. The baker subsequently went bankrupt, lost his business and home, and had to move to Adelaide to find work to support his family.[8]

To be white Anglo-Saxon protestant was the norm in these troubled times, and those who did not conform to this ideal were branded traitors. There was a necessity to blame someone for this war, and those who could not be accepted within that norm became the scapegoats.

One other attitude which emerged following the end of the war was that of the returned soldiers. On their return many of them decided to settle on the land and take up farming. Although some had been allotted land in good districts, many had been offered land which they considered to be of a poorer quality. They immediately began to question the propriety of their having to accept "land of doubtful quality"[9] on which they would have to work for many years to make a decent living. They considered this an injustice, especially since there were "large tracts of land in the most prosperous portions of the State owned by persons of enemy origin who did nothing, directly or indirectly, to help in the winning of the war".[10]

In their bitter resentment and anti-German attitude it became convenient for them to overlook the fact that these 'Germans' had struggled for many years to establish what now appeared to be prosperous farms, having initially started with the bare necessities and a determined attitude to succeed. It was even suggested "that all lands belonging to the disloyal element of the population should be purchased from the owners at their own income tax valuation, and made available to ex-A.I.F land-seekers."[11] Within this setting it was also convenient for them to overlook the fact that some of these owners were children of the original settlers who had been encouraged to emigrate to South Australia specifically to work the land and assist in the economic growth of the colony.

The Education Act of 1916 which prohibited the teaching of the German language in Lutheran schools, and the subsequent closing of forty nine Lutheran schools on 30th June, 1917, meant the students had to transfer to the nearest State school where the teaching medium was entirely in English. This proved to be quite a set-back for those children whose parents spoke only German at home. It was also a difficult time for the teachers since the Lutheran pastors stated that the children should still continue to learn the German language and absorb German ideas in the home. Education Authorities were concerned about this influence and stated that:

> *'While the State is striving to teach these children British and Australian ideas in English during the school week the fact remains that their spiritual teachers whether loyal or not, continue to imbue their charges with religious tenets and instruction and to mould their religious thoughts and speech in a language foreign to that of their native land...'*[12]

The use of the German language for Church services was also curtailed and the Lutheran Church attempted, unsuccessfully, to have this decision rescinded, stating that German was the original language of Lutheranism. The printing of literature in German was also banned. Church periodicals and German newspapers now had to be produced in the English language. It was claimed by those who criticised the use of the German language that "these publications frequently reproduce stories and articles wholly harmless in the abstract but which are well calculated to keep alive German ideas, ideals and sympathies."[13]

This anti-German feeling did not disappear at the end of the war. In fact, during July, 1920, the importation of any printed matter in the German language, intended for use by the Lutheran Church in Australia, was prohibited. This Customs Proclamation No. 2 was published in the Commonwealth Gazette No.59 of the 8th July, 1920, page 944.[14]

The fear of subversive material infiltrating into the minds of so-called pro-Germans was still very strong. People who had been interned during World War One were released after the cessation of hostilities and a 'watch' kept on their activities. Reports were submitted as to where they went, to whom they spoke, and in some instances what they actually said was recorded, supposedly verbatim. These reports were filed periodically during the 1920s and 1930s and proved useful to the authorities at the outbreak of World War Two in 1939.

But gradually, during the years between the two wars, the tension began to ease somewhat and many Australians of German descent renewed their ties with people in Germany. Many Australian-Germans who had relatives over there, felt the necessity of helping to relieve the hardship and suffering which was being experienced throughout the whole of Germany. An organisation called the South Australian European Relief Fund came into operation just prior to 1920 and Field-Marshall von Hindenburg was the patron in Germany. "Gifts of money, clothing and flour were received from people of German descent in all parts of South Australia and were despatched by German ships to the address of Pastor Loeffler in Hamburg."[15]

The need to retain their ties with Germany was still very strong, and the temptation to compare the political worth of both Germany and Britain, even after Germany's loss, must have been difficult to avoid for some people. Many Australian-Germans must have felt torn between a loyalty to Australia, their land of birth or adoption, and Germany, the land from which their religion, language and culture had been transferred, especially since the Lutheran Church continued to maintain its ties with Germany.

Price suggests that after 1928 the Nazi Party's new theory that "blood overrides nationality and that the German race was destined to conquer the world".[16] was the reason for the increase in South Australian German activities. He states that many "associated organisations began to propagate the more aggressive pan-Germanic theory".[17]

Two such organisations, the S.A.A.D.V. (the South Australian General German Club) and Die Bruecke, a German newspaper printed in Sydney, were considered to be at the centre of this new movement, and anyone identifying themselves with these two organisations was presumed to have Nazi sympathies.

He considers the next group were those "who, well acquainted with Nazi ambitions, expressed their interest by attending Dr. Becker's film evenings and by taking part in the pro-German activities of various Australian-German societies".[18]

The last group, according to Price, were those on the outskirts of the South Australian German community "who failed to realize the full implications of the Nazi Volksgedanke[19] but were anxious to retain the pre-1914 policy of fostering the German language and culture".[20]

In my opinion, Price fails to consider that many may have been interested in the first two groups for reasons other than political. How can he be so sure that everyone was aware of the political bias of those groups? He tends to lump all German descendants together as pro-Nazi in inclination when the majority were simply interested in their German origins. There were many who were not well acquainted with Nazi ambitions, but whose interest in Germany at that time was due to religious and family historical events.

In retrospect it is all too easy to consider these people as naive, since we now know the extent to which those in power in Germany were prepared to go in their efforts to purify the German nation. The rest of the world was unaware of Hitler's territorial ambitions. He was a master at firing enthusiasm and a magician in the art of mass hysteria. Many people were swept along in that tide of enthusiasm, both in Germany and in countries to which Germans had migrated. The following quote from a South Australian publication in 1933, emphasizes this admiration for Hitler's actions during the earlier part of his political career.

> *'That a man of the people, the son of a junior customs officer, a private in the German army during the World War, could within a few years, create a movement to which millions flocked, that he won victories in one election after another ... all this is phenomenal, and shows him to be a man of destiny.*[21]

In South Australia much pro-German activity came to the fore in the years immediately preceding the 1936 Centenary Celebrations. As later events show, it was a period of time which had far reaching effects on many unsuspecting Australians of German descent.

During November, 1933, information was received by the Commonwealth Investigation Branch that a branch of the Nazi Party was being formed in Australia by Dr. J. Becker, who was living in South Australia and had arrived from Germany six years earlier. Becker practised medicine at Tanunda, but as his Marburg degree was not recognized by the B. M.A., he was obliged to practise unregistered.

The organisation was to foster German interests within Australia in the form of a propaganda society distributing leaflets and books, and showing films on German cultural life. But this organisation did not become popular and Becker, who had tried to establish a core group within the Australian-German areas of the State, gained minimal support and was seemingly stigmatized by many residents of Australian-German nationality.[22]

Becker had been instrumental in the formation of Die Deutsche Fortbildungsverein (The German Educational Society) in 1935, which was ostensibly a non-political organisation for Australian citizens of German descent, which met to discuss German culture; history, literature and music. The society held its meetings at Tanunda in the Sunday School Hall of St. John's Lutheran Church and in a room behind Mattiske's store. These meetings occasionally included lectures by visiting Germans and film evenings of German cultural interest. The film shows were open to the public and held in the Tanunda Institute. The society's circulating library of approximately three hundred books included literature on non-political topics such as German life, achievements, virtues and love of the Homeland, as well as literature intent on educating readers in the ideals of National Socialist Germany. This society was disbanded prior to the outbreak of World War Two.

A security report compiled toward the end of World War Two on the activities of this society suggests it was created as part of a plan for the unification of German Folk-Groups abroad, but it appears to have been influential only within the Tanunda district.[23]

'Although its activities as known seem to point to propaganda purposes only, it is unlikely that other aspects were neglected.

Indications of these processes exist, as several youths of German descent were sent to Germany with recommendations from Dr. Becker, to acquire training of some kind – Anton Semmler to an engineering school, Bert Schulz to learn printing, and others. Persons travelling to Germany from the Tanunda district were well aware that their good reception was assured if they were recommended by Dr. Becker, and it is probable that his recommendation was contingent on their membership of a German organisation incorporated in the Folk-Group, such as the Fortbildungsverein may be taken to be.[24]

During 1935 the German-Australian Centenary Committee was established. The reason for its formation was to promote friendly relations between the people of British and German birth or descent during the 1936 South Australian Centenary celebrations. The first meeting was held at the German Club in Adelaide and Heinrich Krahwinkel was elected chairman. Krahwinkel had arrived in Australia from Germany during 1913 and had subsequently become naturalised in 1920. The two Lutheran Synods were also represented on this committee through Pastors J. J. Stolz (U.E.L.C.A.) and O.S. Nichterlein (E.L.C.A.).[25]

The specific aims of this society were, firstly, to restore the German place names of Klemzig, Hahndorf and Lobethal which had been changed to Gaza, Ambleside and Tweedvale by the Nomenclature Act of 1917. Public meetings were held in the three towns to elicit support for the venture. Through the efforts of the Honorable Hermann Homburg, who made representations in Parliament, a Nomenclature Bill was passed and became law in December, 1935.[26]

The second aim of the Committee was to honour the German composer of the 'Song of Australia' Carl Linger, by collecting funds to erect a memorial at the West Terrace Cemetery in Adelaide. On

17th June, 1936, the Premier of South Australia, the Honorable R. L. Butler, unveiled this memorial and paid tribute to the composer who died in 1862.[27] He also paid tribute to the many other German colonists "in grateful memory of their steadfast, energetic and helpful work in the founding and development of our State".[28] Since the money for the monument had been raised by public subscriptions by arrangement with the Adelaide newspaper, The Advertiser, the ceremony was partly in English and German. This helped to attract a large number of English people who also wished to show their appreciation.

Thirdly, it was the intention of the Committee to renovate the Klemzig Cemetery, burial place of some of South Australia's German pioneers. This they did, and on 29th August, 1936, a memorial to the first German Lutheran settlers in Australia was unveiled at this cemetery by the Governor of South Australia, Sir Winston Dugan.[29] The General Presidents of the two Lutheran Synods each gave addresses. Pastor J.J. Stolz, of the U.E.L.C.A. Synod, stated that everyone "owed a debt of gratitude to the pious little group that had founded the village of Klemzig ninety eight years ago".[30] The gratitude of the present generation of Lutherans "was joined with the promise of their faithful devotion to God, to the State and to the Empire of which they had become a part".[31] Pastor W. Janzow, of the E.L.C.A. Synod, emphasized the freedom which everyone in Australia shared. He stressed the fact that "there was no greater misfortune for a State than religious intolerance."[32] He believed that religious freedom would always keep a nation peaceful and harmonious, and stated that "from such freedom springs the feeling of loyalty towards a government which understands how to protect the most sacred rights of its subjects".[33]

During the ceremony wreaths were laid by descendants of Pastor Kavel and from both Lutheran Synods, by the German-Australian

Centenary Committee, and from the Party Organisation of the N.S.D.A.P. (National Socialist German Workers' Party). The latter was a laurel wreath tied with a ribbon on which was displayed the swastika.

A report of this event in the newspaper, Die Bruecke, concluded with the statement that "the day of the unveiling of this monument in the old Klemzig Cemetery will live long in the memory of the Deutschtum of Australia"[34] Little did anyone realize that three years hence the true significance of that occasion would be misconstrued and everyone connected with the planning and organisation of it would be under suspicion as Nazi sympathisers.

The South Australian German Historical Society developed from the German-Australian Centenary Committee during 1937, and a sub-committee, the Klemzig Cemetery Trust, was responsible for the upkeep of the pioneer cemetery.[35] Membership of the Historical Society was open to all German-Australians, and also to all other persons interested in the welfare of German-Australians. The Society continued to maintain friendly relations as previously, and extended this aim to include communication between Australian descendants and their relatives in Germany. Through the encouragement of the Society various members of German-Australian families visited Klemzig and the villages in Brandenburg when they travelled overseas to Europe.

The following information, drawn up by security regarding officials of the two societies between 1935 and 1939, gives their view of the involvement of these men in their German heritage.

Krawinkel; President. Honorary Consul for Germany during 1929-31. Married the daughter of Hermann Homburg. Decorated by the Deutsches Ausland-Institut in 1937 for his services in fostering German-Australian relations. Close associate of Dr. J. H. Becker.

Dr. A. J. Schulz; Honorary Treasurer 1935-39. Born in South Australia, 1883, of German parents. Spent 1907-09 in Europe gaining Degree of Doctor of Philosophy at the University of Zurich in Switzerland. Appointed Principal of the Teachers' Training College in South Australia in 1910.

Pastor J.J. Stolz; Committee member 1935-39 and member of the Klemzig Cemetery Trust. Born 1878 in South Australia of German father and South Australian born mother of German descent. Spent 1895-99 at Neuendettelsau Mission Seminary in Bavaria. President-General of U.E.L.C A. Synod.

Buring; Committee member 1935-39. Born 1872 in South Australia of German parents. Managing Director of Buring and Sobels winery.

A. Borchers; Committee member 1935-36. Born 1868 in Germany and emigrated to Australia 1889. Member of a Communistic colony which attempted to establish itself in Paraguay. Returned to Australia prior to 1914. Revived the German Club after 1914-18 War. President of German Club till 1935: opposed admission of Nazi Party members because of personal dislike of Dr. Becker. Resigned after 1935 when, according to Security reports, the Nazi Party gained control of the Club.

Pastor O.S. Nichterlein; Committee member 1935-39, also member of Klemzig Cemetery Trust. Born 1876 in South Australia of German/German-descended parents. Held influential position in E. L.C. A.

C. Kriewaldt; Committee member 1935-39, also member of Klemzig Cemetery Trust. Born 1908 in Australia of German descent. Educated in America and returned to Australia in 1923. Barrister and Solicitor. Member of Executive Committee of E.L.C.A.

G. E. Nitschke; Committee member 1935-39, also member of Klemzig Cemetery Trust. Born 1884 in Australia of German descent. Representative for Hahndorf. Farmer.

Wiedenhofer; Committee member 1935-39, also member of Klemzig Cemetery Trust. Born approximately 1867 in South Australia of German descent. Representative for Klemzig. President of Klemzig Institute Committee. Manager of Lion Timber Mills.

Dr. C.C. Jungfer; Committee member 1935-39. Born 1900 in South Australia of German descent. Medical Practitioner. Representative for Lobethal. Visited Germany in 1938. Active in all local affairs at Lobethal.

J.F.W. Schulz; Committee member 1938. Born 1883 in South Australia of German descent. Lutheran School teacher prior to closing of schools during World War One. Representative for Tanunda. Part owner and manager of Auricht's Printing Office printers for the Lutheran Church. Author of booklets in 'German-Australian' dialect'. Well-known identity and prominent in all local affairs.

Pfeiffer; Committee member 1937-39. Born 1908 in Germany and arrived in Australia 1927. Not naturalised (as at 1943). President, German Club 1937-39. Employed at General Motors Holdens. Correspondent of a Berlin paper, Der Brief.

Starke; Committee member 1937. Born 1908 in Germany and arrived in Australia 1927. Stuetzpunktleiter (leader of a support group) of the N.S. D.A. P., Adelaide 1933-36. Press Chief for Australia of the Auslands Organisation (Overseas Organisation) of the N.S. D.A. P. 1934-36.

Homburg; Secretary 1938-39. Born 1910 in South Australia of German descent. Daughter of Hon. Hermann Homburg, prominent Solicitor of Adelaide and former Attorney-General of South Australia. Visited Germany with her mother in 1937. Represented the South Australian German Historical Society at the Congress of Germans from Abroad. Closely associated with Paul Beckmann, Acting German Consul in Adelaide, 1939.

B.H. Teusner; born approximately 1908 in South Australia. Solicitor. In July 1939 he was asked to accept the position of Representative for Tanunda. Prominent in all local affairs at Tanunda.[36]

With the outbreak of war in 1939, this Society went into voluntary recess.

The Historical Society also maintained a close association with various German singing groups in South Australia and invited them to sing at various functions. One of these, the Tanunda Liedertafel which was established in 1861, was a "very old, very German, singing club whose members belonged chiefly to the long-settled German families of the Barossa district".[37] The conductor and driving force behind the high standard of singing of this group was Fritz Homburg, brother-in-law of H. Krawinkel. On the occasion of the Centenary celebrations in 1938 of the arrival of the first Lutheran settlers to South Australia, the Tanunda Liedertafel provided a program of well-known German folk songs at the Tanunda Institute. This program was transmitted by the Australian Broadcasting Commission to Klemzig in Germany and a program was received from Klemzig, Germany, shortly afterwards. "The reception was very clear. One heard greetings from Klemzig to the Klemzig people in far Australia. A choir also sang songs. The transmission closed with the chiming of the Klemzig church bells".[38] After the close of transmission another musical program, including community Singing of German folk songs, was offered for the assembled group. J. F.W. Schulz was the program announcer.

Societies and Clubs continued to maintain a link with Germany. The Sued Australische Allgemeine Deutsche Verein (South Australian General German Club) was an old established institution which represented the most respectable view of Germanism in South Australia. According to Security reports, there was a change in political attitude within the Club during 1934-35. There were also some personality clashes between Dr. Becker and other members of the Club. Prior to this control of the association had been in the hands of elderly Germans who had no enthusiasm for the New Germany.[39]

From 1937 until the outbreak of World War Two, the political climate apparently changed to support the propaganda work of Hitler's Germany and, according to a report titled 'National Socialism in Australia',[40] the German Club was considered a propaganda centre since "the most important offices were filled either by Nazis or Nazi supporters".[41] Therefore, anyone with even the remotest connection to this Club was considered worthy of investigation by the Commonwealth Authorities during the pre-war years of Fifth-Columnist hysteria.

In 1937 the German Consulate was established in Adelaide, and Dr. Seger took office as the new Consul, together with his secretary, P. Beckmann. In March, 1939, Beckmann took over as Acting Consul when Seger returned to Sydney.[42] It appears, from reports and newspaper articles, that at this time of strained relations between Britain and Germany, the Consul and his Secretary were determined to increase the fervour of South Australian Deutschtum. On the other hand, the Security officials watching and noting these events, may have taken what could have been innocent social/ historical occasions and enthusiasm for the 'old country', as increased fervour for Nazism. During those pre-war years, Security officials obviously watched any associations and groups who had an interest in German affairs, with some degree of suspicion.

Films and printed matter on German life were distributed liberally to Clubs and Associations and individuals, including Lutheran ministers. The recipients saw this as a cultural link with their past, and Krawinkel stated that "German-Australians were always delighted to see in the German press matter dealing with themselves".[43]

Die Bruecke, the German language newspaper published by German Australian Publications Ltd., in Sydney, was considered by Security as "the official propaganda organ of the Nazi Party in Australia".[44] Reports supplied to this newspaper were written with the intention of "creating racial consciousness among the German-descended population by stressing the peculiarity and the superiority of their characteristics".[45] Wilton and Bosworth consider that throughout the long history of the ethnic press, and particularly during the interwar period, "such papers often had a definite political colour ... anti-fascist communities, socialists, or anarchists tried to ... rally Italian migrants to their cause ... Die Bruecke proclaimed the virtues of Hitler's Germany".[46]

Die Bruecke had a poor circulation in South Australia and one might conclude from this that the South Australian Germans were not as interested in the political issues of Deutschtum as the N.S.D.A.P. officials in Australia had hoped they would be. Since the

Lutheran Church was already supplying many of these people with a strong link in all things German, they possibly felt their allegiance should be to Church publications rather than secular German newspapers. The editor of Die Bruecke was aware, however, of the influence which the Lutheran ministers had on the German-Australian members of their flock, and therefore kept in close contact with many of them.

During 1934, the names of six Lutheran Church members were submitted to the German Consul General in Sydney, Dr. Asmis, as being suitable reporters for Die Bruecke in South Australia. These names were submitted by Pastor J.J.Stolz of the U.E.L.C.A. Synod in Adelaide, and Schulz was one of those considered suitable.[47] No doubt this was because of his involvement in the printing and publication of German-Australian secular and religious papers and books at Auricht's Printing Office in Tanunda. Schulz did not take up the offer because he was not sufficiently interested in the success of the paper and because of his own work commitments.

One other German language newspaper, The Queensland Herald, published by Karl Reber of Brisbane, had a fairly wide circulation among the German-descended population of South Australia, particularly after 1929 when Reber bought the publication rights to Die Australische Zeitung from Auricht's Printing Office and incorporated it with The Queensland Herald.[48]

Schulz was interested in collecting information about Germany and German affairs, not only because it was part of his job at Auricht's Printing Office when they published Die Australische Zeitung, but because he was interested in his German heritage.

One of his hobbies was making 16mm movie films of interest to the local Barossa Valley communities. Recording visits made to Adelaide and the Barossa Valley by notable Germans was obviously of great concern to him as he knew these films would be in demand at local fund raising evenings.

During the years 1925 till the outbreak of World War Two in 1939, many such Germans visited Australia. Captain Hans Bertram made a visit to Tanunda on 5th October, 1932. This followed his recuperation from the crash, on the north-west coast of Australia, of his ill-fated propaganda flight for the Reich in the Junkers sea plane 'Atlantis'. After visiting places of interest around Tanunda, he was officially welcomed by Fritz Homburg and a crowd of local residents at the Tanunda Memorial Hall. Captain Bertram then spoke to the people about his experiences following the crash landing of his plane until he and his mechanic, Klaussmann, were rescued.[49]

Baron von Oertzen, a representative for Auto Union, the German company which manufactured D.K.W. cars and motorcycles, visited South Australia during 1937-38. He led the German racing team at Lobethal on 27th December, 1937. The Baron was accompanied by his wife Irene, Ewald Kluge, a racing driver, and Wagner, a mechanic. The main aim of this visit was to establish interest in D.K.W. cars and motorcycles with the view to establishing an industry in Australia.[50]

The Australian Lecture Tour of Count Felix von Luckner from 2nd-24th July, 1938, was one which left a lasting impression in the minds of all who saw him. With his wife, the Countess, and his tour manager, Mr. R. F. Chapman, the Count visited Sydney, Wagga Wagga, Melbourne, Colac, Geelong, Adelaide, Caulfield, Albury, Henty, and then returned to Sydney to board the yacht, 'Seeteufel', for their return to Germany.[51] While staying in Adelaide the couple made a short visit to the Tanunda district and the Count spoke to the local residents about his experiences as a sailor during World War One. At that time he was Captain of the German raider, 'Seeadler' to which fifty seven ships fell victim. Fritz Homburg welcomed the

Count to Tanunda, the Tanunda Liedertafel sang German songs, and at the close of von Luckner's speech, J. F.W. Schulz thanked him on behalf of those assembled.[52]

According to Security reports, it has been suggested that von Luckner was sent by the Auslands Organisation of the N.S.D.A.P. to create friendly relations between German and Australian Returned Soldiers; to emphasize the desire for friendship between Germany and England, and to encourage a sense of being a part of the 'Greater Germany' among Germans and persons of German descent.[53]

F. W. Schulz filmed von Luckner's visit to Tanunda and was part of the interested group of residents who attended the special functions arranged for the three mentioned German visitors to South Australia.

The question of assimilation and absorption is important during this period of time between the two World Wars. Much of the social and political life of German-born and German-descended people was observed and recorded by the Military Authorities at the outbreak of World War Two, used as evidence of pro-German or pro-Nazi sympathy. Many German-Australians, in particular the elderly members of the family, had not attempted to learn English. This indifferent attitude was viewed by the authorities as an admission of neglect in their duty toward Australian citizenship and a sign of pro-German sentiment.

Gradually it became more difficult for the German-Australian community to maintain its duality. The German language was slowly losing the battle for survival. With the introduction of instruction entirely in English within the Lutheran Schools, and the teaching of German as a separate subject rather than a teaching medium, the absorption of these people and the loss of their foreign characteristics soon became noticeable. It appears that the forces which paved the way for absorption were stronger than those for maintaining Deutschtum.

Nevertheless, on the eve of World War Two, the German-Australian community of the Barossa Valley region still formed a very distinct group within South Australia.

***

1. I.A. Harmstorf, 'They worked hard and prayed long' in The Bulletin, July 10, 1976, p. 35.
2. The Sunday Times, Sydney, November 30, 1919.
3. I.A. Harmstorf, 'They worked hard and prayed long' in The Bulletin, July 10, 1976, p .35.
4. AA: SA 22156 Loxton Royal Commission.
5. Ibid.
6. Ibid.
7. Ibid.
8. Verbal communication from member of Loxton community.
9. AA: SA 22156 Loxton Royal Commission.
10. Ibid.
11. Ibid.
12. AA: SA 1166 Lutheran Schools. Proposal to re-open.
13. Ibid.
14. AA: SA 254 Lutheran Publications in German Language, 1920.
15. AA: SA 20418 Lutheran Church.
16. C.A. Price, German Settlers in South Australia, P.75.
17. Ibid, p. 75.
18. Ibid, p. 75.
19. 'Volksgedanke' - Nazi philosophy.
20. C.A. Price, German Settlers in 'South Australia', p. 75.

21. The Christian Book Almanac, 1933, p. 56.
22. AA: SA 2049 Nazi Party in South Australia.
23. AA: SA 20029 Fortbidungsverein (German Educational Society) 1934 - 1944.
24. Ibid.
25. AA: SS 1550 German Historical Society of South Australia, 1935 - 1943.
26. Ibid.
27. Ibid.
28. Ibid. Part of a translation from Die Bruecke, June 27, 1936.
29. Ibid. part of a translation from Die Bruecke, September 5, 1936.
30. Ibid.
31. Ibid.
32. Ibid.
33. Ibid.
34. AA: SS 1550 German Historical Society of South Australia, 1935-1943. Part of a translation from Die Bruecke, September 5, 1936.
35. Ibid.
36. AA: SS 1150 German Historical Society of South Australia, 1935-1943, pp. 3-4.
37. Ibid, p. 8.
38. AA: SA 22219 German Short Wave 1934-1939. Part of a translation from Die Bruecke, June 25, 1938.
39. AA: SA 20419 Nationalist Socialist German Workers Party, 1935-1944 (Nazi Party in South Australia).
40. Ibid.
41. Ibid.
42. Ibid.
43. Ibid.
44. AA: SA 20419 Nazi Party in South Australia.

45. AA: SA 1550 German Historical Society of South Australia, 1935-1943.
46. J. Wilton, and R. Bosworth, Old Worlds and New Australia, p. 155.
47. AA: SS 827 J. F. W. Schulz.
48. AA: SA 19561 Schrapel; Walter, Ernst, Erdmann, Aubrey.
49. AA: SA 17203 Visitors from Germany.
50. AA: SA 20418/6 Some Aspects of the N.S.D.A.P. in Australia, S.A. 1943.
51. AA: SA 18121 German Club, 1933-1937.
52. AA: SA 1679 Luckner, Count Felix. 1927-1938.
53. Ibid.

Illustration 6

Illustration 7

4

J. F. W. Schulz: Internment in World War Two

'Where no wood is, there the fire goeth out:
So where there is no tale—bearer, the strife ceaseth.'
Proverbs 26:20

On 3rd September, 1939, England declared war against Nazi Germany. This meant that Australia was once again at war with Germany, the homeland of a number of South Australians, or their parents or grandparents. Early in the war the National Security Act was passed which gave the Federal Government increased powers to deal with people who were seen to be friendly toward the enemy, or who endangered National security. These powers included the right to seize and intern. When introducing this Bill to the Federal Parliament, the Prime Minister, Mr. Menzies, said "there must be as little interference with individual rights as is consistent with concerted national effort".[1]

Many members were critical of aspects of the legislation, fearing that it would lead to abuses of power and discrimination against people of German descent. Maurice Blackburn, M. H. R., emphasized the deprivation of personal liberty involved with this Bill when he remarked:

> 'This Bill takes away the right of Habeas Corpus. Neither Parliament nor the Judiciary have any check upon Ministers ... In war no man can be trusted to be fair and just. The only thing that kept Magistrates from losing their heads in the 1914 War was that they sat, not in secret, but in open Court. There is no reason why we should not have open trials.'[2]

Security officers were granted authority to search and arrest anyone under suspicion using evidence based on hearsay and gossip. This authorisation was worded as follows:

> 'Being satisfied by information on Oath that there is reasonable ground for suspecting that a war offence has been or is being committed, and that evidence of the commission of the offence is to be found at the premises of one ... of ... in the State of South Australia, I, the undersigned, one of His Majesty's Justices of the Peace in and for the State of South Australia hereby authorize you ... a commissioned officer in the Defence Force ... to enter the said premises at any time or times within one month from the date hereof, if necessary by force, and to search the same, and every person found therein, and to seize any article found in the said premises or on any such person which you have reasonable ground for believing to be evidence of the commission of such an offence.'[3]

In the fearful and suspicious atmosphere of the early war years, rumours were rife. 'Fifth columnists' supposedly abounded everywhere. The concerned public were encouraged to inform on any incident which they saw as unusual, knowing full well that no redress to themselves would follow should their information be false. In many instances informers committed perjury in an attempt to settle old scores against persons who had at one time or another slighted them. The Federal Minister, Thorby, made the following statement in The Advertiser, 15th May, 1940, in an attempt to encourage people to do what was right for the country.

> *'Australians should not hesitate to tell tales on neighbours they suspect of acting in a manner detrimental to the welfare of the country. People should unhesitatingly report it to the authorities. Some people will not give information to the police as they fear they might have to appear in open Court. They can, therefore, give the information to me.'*[4]

The Lutheran Church came under attack because of its religious ties with Germany. Immanuel College, the secondary school of the U.E.L.C.A. Synod, situated in Jeffcott Street, North Adelaide, was often referred to as "the German College".[5] Trainee ministers of the Lutheran Church invariably completed their Seminary studies in Germany as there were no facilities here at that time in which they could receive the equivalent theological education. The overall aim was "to secure ... connection with Lutheran theology, and, on the whole, with the rich intellectual and spiritual life-stream of the German Lutheran mother-Church."[6] Information given to the Intelligence Department on 'subversive activities' showed that many people were suspicious of people of German descent, and the Lutheran Church.

Members of the Security Service regularly gave talks to various associations and groups on topics such as, 'Security', 'Espionage in South Australia', 'The Security Service Relative to Aliens', 'Fifth

Column Activities in Australia', and 'Don't Talk Campaigns'.[7] The resulting enthusiasm by many Australians for their country's safety was often so great that many innocent persons were reported as having uttered treacherous remarks or having been seen in suspicious circumstances. People so accused suffered the indignation and rejection of their fellow townsfolk entirely on hearsay alone.

F. W. Schulz was one of those who was reported on by neighbours and other local informers. On Friday, 13th December, 1940, Schulz was arrested at Tanunda. He had just returned from Angaston where he had watched the Tanunda Fire Brigade attempting to extinguish a fire at Mutton Brothers store. A car stopped behind him and a Security Officer stated he would like to inspect Auricht's Printing Office. Two other Officers joined them and the inspection began.

During the search of the Printing Office questions were asked about his associations with Dr. Becker, newspapers he had received from Dr. Becker, and whether he had reprinted material from these papers. In relation to the last question, his denial was met by utter disbelief. The authorities asked questions about the publications of Auricht's Printing Office; his relationship with the Lutheran Church; the mailing lists for his publications, and his son's visit to Germany.

The search party then moved to inspect the study at his private residence. He was asked why he had made a film of Count von Luckner's visit to South Australia, to which he replied that as a show-man who raised funds for charities and local committees, it was his business to get films of universal interest. He said a film of von Luckner, who was instrumental in doing so much harm to shipping during the Great War, would be a drawcard practically anywhere.

A file on the table in his study contained articles of a political nature from newspapers and books. When asked why he kept all those articles, he stated that he read not only ideas he agreed with, but he also liked to study the views of political opponents. A copy of Hitler's Mein Kampf was impounded; Chamberlain's My Struggle For Peace, with its many underlined passages, was passed by.

Following the search he was arrested. The officers allowed him to change his clothes, pack a few essentials and hurriedly explain to his wife and daughter that he was to be detained. He was then driven to Wayville Detention Camp in Adelaide. No accusation had been made directly to him in the course of the search, but he knew what this arrest meant; someone, somewhere, had considered him a threat. He was fifty seven years of age, a respected man, and a community leader. He commented in his diary:

> 'I took my detention philosophically; but it was hard when we passed Marie's home at Nuriootpa.[9] Pastor Chris.Stolz[10] and Hermann Homburg[11] were wonderful when I arrived at Wayville Camp ... Pastor Stolz quickly arranged a bunk for me. A bed knocked together by the inmates, a straw mattress and a blanket. From my bed I see seven barbed wires.'[11]

During the first week of detention his Solicitor, Mr. Harford, arranged for an appeal against the Detention Order. This was the first step in a long line of legal procedures to clear his name and procure his release.

Schulz found it difficult to adjust to his new environment. Wayville Detention Camp, which had formerly been the Wayville Showgrounds prior to being used as a holding centre for detainees, was within a few miles of the centre of Adelaide. Schulz had freely visited Adelaide on many occasions for business or social reasons prior to his detention. Now he was no longer free to travel at will. Each night the events of the previous days would surge through his mind making it difficult to sleep, so he decided to jot those thoughts down and use them to write diary entries each day.

Fritz Homburg,[12] brother of the Hon. Hermann Homburg, was another well-known Tanunda identity who had been arrested and detained. Schulz knew him well. Fritz Homburg managed, possibly through political connections, to procure a National Advisory Committee hearing within one week of being detained, despite the fact that there were approximately thirty internees who had arrived at the Camp before him. He was released within a few days; his detention was just a mistake!

Schulz wrote numerous letters of appeal to the Hon. Mr. R. S. Richards, M.P., Leader of the Opposition in State Parliament but to no avail. On 17th December. 1940, he signed a statement giving notice of objection to his detention.[13] There was an evergrowing feeling of resentment in the Camp over the discrimination in the order of hearings. News filtered through the Camp that one of the detained men was taking information for the Intelligence Department. Another inmate was on the verge of a nervous breakdown.

Schulz was finally heard on 26th February, 1941, some ten weeks after his arrest. His ten witnesses were there to support him. At the conclusion of his hearing, his Solicitors told him he should get a clear discharge, but on 13th March his Solicitor, Harford, called to inform Schulz that he (Harford) was going to Canberra to talk to Spender, Minister for the Army, about the case. Two weeks later, Harford called again at Wayville Camp to see Schulz and report on the Canberra trip. Apparently he had seen Spender, in company with Makin, a South Australian Labor representative and Curtin, Leader of the Labor Party and later Prime Minister, and was awaiting a reply from Spender.

There were long delays involved with these hearings and while waiting for the outcome of his own, he followed the cases of other internees closely. His hopes were raised when Counsel for M. Pohl contested the legality of the long delays, arguing it was contrary to that basis for justice, the system of 'habeas corpus'. But the Minister for the Army had appointed this special Advisory Committee to consider the facts submitted, and to make recommendations to the Minister as to what should be done. Any delays which had occurred to date were supposedly beyond his control. In essence, the Ministers were given great powers which were contrary to British Justice. Here it was a case of military rule overriding the legal system. Normal legal rights had been diminished and civil rights were impaired. The Government had overreacted and allowed military regulations to be used against ordinary citizens.

Schulz's detention had, of course, limited his chance of election since the Labor Party could not champion the cause of a candidate who was considered by the Military Authorities to be detrimental to the safety of the country. He commented in his diary that he appeared to have committed the unpardonable sin of daring to contest the political seat of Angas against a minister of the Crown!

> *'As God is my judge I have never uttered nor harboured disloyal sentiments. I may have criticised adversely our political, financial and social institutions, but always with a view to improving conditions. And now I am told that the fee will be one hundred pounds to fight myself out of here! To gain my freedom! To go on the stand and convey a message that I feel I must tell! Ah, now we have it! I have the temerity to oppose a sitting member of Parliament! I pray to God that he give me freedom and health!'*[14]

Two days later he wrote: "I feel like chucking in my bundle".[15]

Newspaper reports of the Election results contained interesting comments regarding the campaign in Angas which had been conducted in peculiar circumstances. One newspaper stated that:

> 'British democracy was never better designed or demonstrated than in (recent) elections. ... In one country district, hundreds of voters were allowed to poll their Number One vote for a candidate who, for some time previous to the election, had been detained by the authorities. ... Perhaps never before in Australian politics has such a situation presented itself of a candidate who had neither appeared before his electors nor circulated a policy speech.'[16]

Schulz polled seven hundred and five votes out of a total of three thousand five hundred and ninety seven votes,[17] proving that some members of the community considered him to be a man of substance and worthy of their support even though he had been arrested and detained by the authorities.

While in Wayville Camp, Schulz observed the characteristics of the various cultural groups and shared an affinity with some more than others. The exercising space of the detention area measured twenty five yards two feet by six yards one foot and four inches, and within this space twenty five to thirty men moved and mingled together. In this situation, as he astutely remarked, "nationality and political creed soon faded into the background and you learned to evaluate the man".[18]

He liked the group of Italians from Port Pirie who were there when he first arrived at Wayville. They were, on the whole, quiet and considerate, and did not push their political views on to other inmates. But the second group, who arrived in March, 1941, and to whom he referred as 'the Hindley Street Italians' because they lived in cheap boarding houses and hotels in Hindley Street, were a different breed entirely. He found them loud mouthed, coarse, and their personal hygiene left much to be desired, so much so that two weeks after their arrival, bedding and mattresses from their cubicles were removed and burnt, and a 'de-bugging' operation of the whole Camp was necessary.

When the original group of Italians were sent to Tatura Camp in Victoria, for the duration of the war, Schulz found it difficult to cope with the other Italians. As a family man he was used to living in a clean and well cared for home, and since the beginning of his detention, he had made every effort to improve the inside of his cubicle to boost his morale and give himself a sense of purpose.

The atmosphere of apprehension and uncertainty within the Camp was beginning to show, and Schulz's diary entries revealed his own depressed attitude.

> *'30th April: The last day of the month. Some of us were hoping for a decision on our appeal by today. The seriousness of the war no doubt overshadows everything else. We have been forgotten.*[19]
>
> *2nd May: I am now here twenty weeks—five months, and a whisper is around that a batch of 'Germans' is due for Tatura at an early date!*[20]
>
> *4th May: Sergeant Major Inwood tells me the news — Tatura this week.*[21]

One can only speculate regarding the effect this news had on Schulz. If we base our speculations on the entries in his diary, then we would be correct in assuming that this news was utterly devastating to his morale as no entries were made for one month. The internment order meant he had been found 'guilty'; that he would be removed from family and friends; that he was to be kept and classed with 'aliens' when he was Australian born. Although he made no diary entries, he did write a letter to the Hon. R. S. Richards, Leader of the Opposition, in which he stated:

> 'I have been informed by the Camp Commandant that within a few days I am to be transferred from here to the Internment Camp at Tatura, Victoria. This means in effect that the Committee that heard my appeal did not believe the evidence given by me on oath. I desire to assure you, Sir, that I did not commit perjury when giving my evidence before the Committee. Here at Wayville my name is entered as a German, I believe. I will never change my name, but I am not a German. I was born here fifty eight years ago and this is my country. I may differ with the powers that are as to the methods to be adopted as to our country's future welfare, but even my further internment is not going to shift me from doing whatever is in my power to prevent this country ever having to suffer a similar crucifixion to that of the innocents of small European nations.
>
> We have here at Wayville just now an internee who has already been at Tatura for a term. From him I learn that so far as he knows there are no more than half a dozen Australian born internees at that Camp. Am I to stay there for the duration? I have offered my services to the authorities as a hospital orderly whenever I might be sent. Surely I cannot be considered dangerous serving in that capacity?'[22]

Schulz had written a restrained and dignified letter questioning the reasons for his impending move to Tatura. He had every right to question the authorities, considering the lack of detrimental evidence produced at his Hearing. The reasons for his continued detention had not been specified and his character witnesses had spoken highly of him. Consequently he could not understand why he was to be sent to a Camp which had only a few Australian born citizens in it.

Richards' response to the letter shows no sympathy for the situation Schulz was in. Richards wrote "I have no knowledge of the intentions of the authorities, but I will forward your letter to the responsible Minister asking if any information can be given on the points raised by you."[23]

It is interesting to speculate on other thoughts which must have gone through Schulz's mind when he heard about Tatura. During those months at Wayville he had plenty of time to think about issues preceding his arrest. He and his family thought the reason for this was a political one. They thought that perhaps there was some resentment by Liberal party members when he changed sides. There was also the suggestion that neighbours and fellow townsfolk who had been at the receiving end of his 'wrath at one time or another, may have informed on him to the authorities as a pro-Nazi sympathiser, particularly because of his interest in the local German groups.

Then, of course, there was his late realization of 'guilt by association' with Dr. Becker, a point he made in his diary jottings while at Wayville.

> 'My associations with Dr. Becker in the light of present events were unfortunate ... I met him almost daily either at the Post Office or when the train arrived with the evening paper. We had many arguments on political matters. Early in Hitler's career I subscribed to many of his views and actions. I read Mein Kampf and this book more than anything helped me to evaluate its author as the unscrupulous schemer he is ...

> *Germany under Hitler is a people without a belief in God, in Christianity, but with a belief only in force. We must fight an ideology that resolves itself into a pagan worship of force.*'24

Information had filtered through Camp that one detentionist had been approached to act as stool-pigeon, and another had been asked to supply information which would lead to the apprehension of more citizens. So Schulz and the others were no safer inside the barbed wires than they were in their own home towns. Their conversations were still being repeated to the authorities and misinterpreted to all intents and purposes.

The journey to Tatura via Melbourne was long and tiring. The group of nineteen men who left Wayville Camp on the evening of 2nd June, 1941, experienced some unpleasant and undignified situations en route to their destination. They were paraded before the public as prisoners under armed guard, and in one instance were marched into one of the 'left luggage' rooms with iron grilles on two sides, while the officials sorted out some confusion about their onward travel arrangements.

The truck which took them to Broadmeadows, almost twelve miles from Melbourne, had no seats and was closed in at the back, which did not allow room for standing. So they squatted, knelt, lay about, and made the best of a bad journey. The midday meal was over when they arrived at Broadmeadows, and they had not eaten since breakfast at Ballarat. Guards with fixed bayonets marched them to the Messroom where they were offered cold chops and lukewarm tea. They were herded to and fro like animals and treated as criminals. No privacy was granted them and they were even escorted to the toilets under armed guard.

The following morning the group, which had now increased in size, boarded a train for Murchison East, and after a further truck ride of twenty or so miles, reached Tatura at midday. The additions to the group were Tatura internees who had been before the Tribunal in Melbourne.

'Tatura' refers to a series of internment camps which had been established by the Federal Government with the outbreak of World War Two. There were camps for German and Italian P.O.W.'s and for married couples evacuated from Singapore.[25] Schulz was interned at Tatura from June 1941 to April 1942. Being there meant he would be unable to receive visits from his family as he had at Wayville. It also meant the authorities believed he was guilty. As the weeks and months dragged on he felt he would never be released, and thoughts such as these weighed heavily on his mind.

At Tatura there were Germans, Italians, Jewish refugees, including the Dunera[26] group, Jehovah's Witnesses and Seventh Day Adventists. Some were pro-Nazi, others anti-Nazi, and yet others were indifferent toward any form of politics. Schulz found it interesting to meet and talk with these men, some of whom were cultured and educated, and with whom he swapped classical or educational reading material. There were approximately one thousand men in Camps IA and B, which encompassed an area of approximately twenty acres.

Schulz was now living an institutionalized life. He was no longer an individual but part of a mass which was constantly ordered about. Camp life entailed a regular routine and everyone had jobs to do. Each person was responsible for his own bed area and each hut was inspected daily. Schulz had made his area more comfortable on his first day at Tatura. He and one other internee had ingeniously decided to make improvised window panes to take the place of the heavy iron shutters. They did this by soaking drawing paper in boiling dripping, which made the paper transparent and durable. Schulz had also made himself a table and some shelving to house his books and odds and ends.

The entire Camp was controlled by the internees under the supervision of the Camp Commandant and his staff. Work in the kitchen, the bakery, the canteen and the cafes provided a limited number of men with employment. Yet the great majority simply roamed at large. To distract the minds and stimulate the energies of these men, the Camp leaders set about evolving schemes and providing the necessary facilities in various branches of sport. A large area provided by the authorities was fenced and got ready. Here the younger athletic section engaged in handball and football and conducted athletic events: running, putting the shot, etc.

Men with financial means laid down tennis courts, a skittle alley, and the initial preparations for a bowling green were made. Weeks before the tennis courts were ready, players were busy practicing at every vantage point in the Camp. To recompense the promoters of tennis and skittles for their outlay, a small charge was made to players, and the playing areas were usually booked out weeks ahead.

The men also took up gardening to help pass the time. The gardens were well kept despite the difficult physical conditions, and there were no weeds to be seen. Despite the fact that the Camp was laid out on the slope of a small stony hill, this did not deter the men from turning comparative waste land into flourishing gardens. Suitable fertile soil and manure was supplied by the Military Authorities.

Many of the inmates were skilled musicians. A men's choir and orchestra under the conductorship of Dr. Gruber, the former conductor of the Vienna Boys Choir, performed concerts for the internees periodically. Films were hired from Melbourne and moving pictures screened on three successive nights every two weeks as part of the Camp entertainment.

It would be easy to paint a picture of contentment within the Camp at Tatura, but it was not entirely so. For the first time in his life, Schulz was pushed into the close company of different types of people. Many of these internees made an effort to improve their lot, and some were even fortunate enough to have jobs which enabled them to work 'outside'. These were woodcutters, roadmakers and gardeners. But Schulz was not free. He was far from his family, and the only contact he had with them, apart from one visit, was through letters and parcels. Of course the letters were censored and stilted, and contained only local news, but helped him forget what was going on around him. It didn't matter whether the Russians were fleeing before the German avalanche, or whether cities were going up in flames; he would simply unwrap his parcel of tobacco, smoke his pipe of Bauer's mixture, and remember what freedom and home were like.

In the Camp, life had its routine, but the days dragged on and Schulz noted every detail to do with the Camp and the progress of hearings of the other internees in his diary. Any little break in the routine or any turn, expected or unexpected, in the hearings was noted down. The new internees talked of appeals to the authorities and constantly wrote letters. Others, who had already tried every avenue, had given up. Schulz continued to write to the authorities, but the replies were always negative. The timetable for hearings was very slow. A trial expected to take one day might suddenly be unexpectedly delayed. Some internees, arrested after Schulz, were able to have their hearings ahead of those who had been waiting in the Camp for some time.

Hughie Eime, an acquaintance of Schulz's, arrived from Wayville Camp on 6th August bringing with him news from Bert and parcels of cheer from home; tobacco, cigarettes and cigarette papers, fruit and sweets. Thoughts of home and family crowded in on him. The distance between Tatura and Tanunda prevented any regular visits by his family, as they had at Wayville, and he missed them all. But their letters and parcels reminded him that he was not alone. Thinking of those in the whole Camp who had no-one with kind thoughts for them became too much for him, and he sat down and cried.

His health began to deteriorate and he suffered constantly from colds and a sore throat. In one incident he tried hard to overcome the need to go into hospital when he was suffering from a very high temperature, by putting himself to bed and sweating it out. When the weather was bitterly cold he would go to bed to keep warm, and spend most of the day reading, either in bed or seated with a thick blanket wrapped around him. On one occasion he suffered acute dysentery and morphia pills were given as a remedy. On his arrival at Tatura he had weighed fourteen stone four pounds. Eight months after his arrival, he weighed twelve stone ten pounds; a loss of almost two stone. In his case he considered the weight loss beneficial, but to someone of smaller and lighter build, such a loss could have caused permanent damage to their health.

In an attempt to keep his mind active he began reading books on Economics, wrote short articles on various aspects of Camp life as an extension of his diary writing, and learned the art of wood-inlay which was a very exacting task, and time consuming, but which gave him great pleasure.

Others in the Camp did not have the determination to overcome the effects of internment which Schulz had. A number of internees tried to escape. While on timber cutting work outside the Camp one day, three men actually managed to escape, but were found within a day or two. There were later attempts by others, but Schnapps, the Camp dog, barked out a warning to the guards and the intending absconders were soon behind the wires once more. But the escapees were not the only ones punished. With each attempt, the rest of the

Camp suffered punishments; either losing their right to listen to the radio or being allowed to read the daily paper.

The effects of internment on some others was more tragic. Henzel of Hut 20 went mad, and a number of others became decidedly unbalanced. They were unable to cope with the pressures and restrictions placed on them.

For a man accustomed to having some control over his destiny, influence in the community, and a belief that British justice was fair, this internment at Tatura was very hard to take. Then, just when things seemed at their blackest, he received news of transfer to Loveday Internment Camp, Barmera, on the River Murray in South Australia.

The initial notification of transfer caused much excitement. Schulz and three others were advised to be at the gate with their luggage on the morning of Monday, 20th April, 1942. They had not been advised of their destination, and the thought that they might at last be returning to South Australia, kept them in suspense. They had asked to be transferred from Camp One, which was recognized by the Military Authorities as a Nazi Camp. The possibility of transfer to Camp Two was disconcerting, but their doubts were put to rest when they were informed that their Bank Accounts had been transferred from Tatura to Loveday in South Australia. South Australia! The State of their birth! Now at last they would be nearer their families.

The attitude of the guards on the journey back impressed Schulz. They were more thoughtful and considerate than on the June 1941 journey to Tatura. Now the group were treated more as victims of circumstance than as criminals.

Schulz found the conditions at Loveday to be most disappointing. They had to live in tents or disused Mess huts, although huts were in the process of being constructed. Each internee was issued with five blankets, and the straw they slept on was changed each month. In several Camps the internees had built brick stoves in the Mess huts, and these stoves were very effective as sources of heating. Schulz shared a Mess hut with thirty seven others. Privacy was a thing of the past.

The majority of the occupants at Loveday Camp were Italians, Japanese and Germans. The atmosphere within his Camp, 14D, was not congenial. A series of minor incidents caused a build-up of tension. Eggs were commandeered by one table at breakfast at the expense of another table; tables, walls etc. in the Mess hall were found decorated in red paint with 'Judenschwien' (Jewish pigs), 'Heil Hitler', and numerous swastikas; timber was stolen to build beds, and news had filtered through that one internee was being held in detention pending trial by civil authorities for the murder of another in Camp 14A.[27] Camp 14D was considered the slackest and least co-operative compound by the authorities, and Schulz had never thought it possible for human beings to behave as many of the individuals did in that compound.

The authorities spent considerable time and effort ensuring a high standard of health and genuine concern for the welfare of the various Camp inmates. There was a Camp Hospital, sick parades were held daily, and a monthly medical examination was obligatory under the National Security (Internment Camp) Regulations; para 28 (6).[28] A dental centre was situated at Group Headquarters. Mess huts were available in all Compounds for indoor recreation and educational purposes, and classes were held in the German and Italian Compounds using books and educational material specifically purchased by the authorities for the internees and P.O. W.'s use.

Schulz spent much of his free time reading from a well-stocked library, and pursued his interest in wood-inlay work at one of the many handicraft workshops within each Compound. Drawing, leatherwork, signwriting, woodworking, bookbinding, model aircraft and toymaking, and the making of fishing rods were other options to those inmates who preferred to keep their minds active during their enforced retirement.

Provision was made for outdoor sports and games, and internees were allowed to play two rounds of golf under escort on the nine hole golf course near Number 10 Compound. Gardening, as a hobby, was encouraged in each of the Compounds and on various occasions, Schulz eagerly anticipated the arrival of seeds and bulbs from his family to ensure a colourful display in his garden plot.

Schulz was given permission to accompany the wood gang and get timber to build himself a bed. He had suffered many inconveniences throughout internment and these had taken their toll on his health, so the thought of a bed to sleep on cheered his spirits. His glasses were also returned to him after a delay of five months. He had handed them in at Tatura and was told they would be ready within one week! During those five months he had been compelled to wear an old pair which were causing eye strain and headaches, and he was almost unable to see anything in bright sunlight. The continued wet and blustery weather during the winter months brought with it the onset of one cold after another for him. "What a life", he wrote in his diary. "Inactivity drawing in its wake morbidity, despair and attendant consequences."[29]

But his internment at Loveday had a brighter side. He was now able to receive visits from his family, and this gave him a new lease on life. Each morning as he took a short walk through the Compound, he would look in the direction of Tanunda. Vineyards were in sight and a homely atmosphere pervaded the air. "Please God", he prayed, "this is the final stage to home".[30]

Many interesting discussions took place among the internees of the various huts. The internees represented all walks of life. They were refugees now, but once they had been in affluent circumstances and had moved in influential circles of society. As they recounted their experiences, the future, in most cases, was designated as hopeless. Particularly that of the refugee who was brought to Australia, his haven of refuge, only to be ultimately interned and refused a hearing before an Appeal Tribunal.[31]

Schulz felt happier at Loveday because he was closer to his home and family. Now they were able to visit him regularly and he felt one step closer to eventual release. His attitude toward the future was positive as this diary entry shows.

> *'I do not lose faith in my country's future. I was reared in a hard school, and even today my family and I are more comfortably situated than were my parents in my childhood days. Though my own government has temporarily bereft me of my freedom, I visualize an ultimate brighter and better future.'*[32]

At Loveday there was hourly paid employment for internees and P.O.W.'s at one shilling per day. A well organised and maintained vegetable garden produced valuable results. At the beginning of 1943 there were 300 acres under cultivation. Vegetables such as marrows, carrots, red beet, onions, potatoes and tomatoes were grown. There were also 9 acres under lucerne for fodder. Seedlings were raised in the nursery for future crops. All vegetables grown were used to supplement the rations supplied by the authorities.

1, 257 internees were engaged daily in paid employment; this was 26.3% of the total number of internees (as at 5th January, 1943).[33] Other areas of paid employment included wood cutting for Camp use; roadmaking which entailed stone quarrying and road construction in and about the Camp; sanitation work involving incinerators, refuse pits, and night soil disposal; soap making; dye works where woollen and cotton garments were dyed the regulation burgundy colour; building projects which included the replacement of tents by huts, brushwood fences, sun shelters and general Camp improvements. Other miscellaneous work included projects such as making watering cans and fly traps, repair of gardening tools, and the construction of Camp and office furniture.

On 30th August, 1942, 25 internees were ordered to pack for elsewhere, presumably Tatura Camp Two, consequently vacancies occurred in various offices and Schulz was offered the position of Works and Wages.[34] He enjoyed this work as it provided him with the mental stimulation he required. It was similar in complexity to work he had done at Auricht's Printing Office. He found it an exacting and challenging job, particularly as it included typing, an area in which he was not entirely proficient. It was some years since he had done such work and he was determined to master it.

Appeals continued to be heard daily but the internees hopes were not met. Schulz reflected how different it was from the day when he had appeared in court and his appeal had been heard; now it was all just considered one huge joke! Various rumours filtered through the Camp regarding reviews of internees cases, but they all despaired of receiving favourable news.

On 13th October, 1942, Schulz had applied by letter to the Deputy Director of Security in Adelaide to appear before the Advisory Committee a second time. He wished to "give further evidence, supplement some of the evidence given ... and to correct some of the evidence as recorded on the twenty odd sheets transcribed from shorthand taken down at the Appeal".[35] This evidence had never been presented to him for his perusal or signature, and he was able to procure a copy later only through the assistance of his Solicitor. Much of the evidence was incorrect and he wished to set the record straight.

Three months later, on 15th January, 1943, he received a reply from the Chief Director of Security in Melbourne, informing him that arrangements were being made for a full investigation of his case and he would be informed of the result in due course. Here at last was a ray of hope. Ten days later he was given the news of a second hearing; it would be an entirely new hearing before an entirely new Appeal Board. He thanked God from the bottom of his heart and felt that justice would now be done.[36]

The Camp inmates were struggling to cope with sweltering heat wave conditions, and Schulz was determined to do everything possible to keep himself healthy. He wrote: "I must be well for the job ahead of me. Practically every day the ambulance is called in and takes men to the hospital. Sun stroke has laid many low and the food is not suited to the weather conditions."[37]

Twenty nine internees made the long and tedious journey to Adelaide by rail for the Hearings and after an hours wait at the Station in Adelaide, were conveyed once more to Wayville Camp; back to where it all began. Two days later Schulz was informed by his Solicitor from Tanunda, Bert Teusner, that it would be impossible for his case to be heard during the week. He would have to go back to Loveday and return to Adelaide the following week. What a blow this must have been for Schulz. Once more the wheels of justice were turning too slow; once more the agony of delay had to be suffered. But at least there was still hope.

Tuesday, 16th February, 1943, was an extremely hot day; 111.1 degrees Fahrenheit in the shade. On that day his second grandchild was born at Tanunda; Bert's first daughter, Elizabeth. Schulz was still at Wayville Camp when he received the news the following day. How he must have wished to have been with his family at this time of happiness. He was forty miles away; so near and yet so far. But his disappointment was tempered with the knowledge that he would soon be returning to Adelaide and would have the chance to clear his name.

Finally, on 30th April and 3rd May, he spent two full days in court, and he commented in his diary:

> 'I am happy about the two days hearings, feeling assured that whatever the result as to my future liberty might be, no evidence was proved during the course of the days that can brand me a traitor to my country.'[38]

Seven months later he had still not heard from the authorities regarding the outcome of the Advisory Committee's recommendation, so he wrote once again to the Right Honorable Dr. Evatt, the Federal Attorney-General, in Canberra. The following day, 8th December, he was advised in a statement from the Deputy Director of Security in South Australia, that his internment was to continue and the Attorney-General had directed that his case be further reviewed in February, 1944.

On 9th December, he wrote two letters, one to Dr. Evatt and one to the Deputy Director of Security in Adelaide, stating in each that "in case the time mentioned for a review of my case has any connection with the South Australian State elections, I desire to state that I had not intended to take part in the election in any form whatsoever."[39]

13th December, 1943. The third anniversary of his internment. Three years behind barbed wire! Two appearances before Advisory Committees, in each case having to wait almost eight months before receiving advice from the Security Department relative to the Advisory Committee's recommendations. What he must have suffered at times, after having testified before God that he was innocent of any act prejudicial to the safety of the Empire and the successful prosecution of the War, can only be surmised. In the meantime, the numerical strength of Camp 14D had dwindled from almost 1,000 men to 255, owing to the exodus of numerous Italians. No doubt the news on 9th September of Italy's unconditional surrender made their release inevitable, whether they were Fascist sympathisers or not.

And so another year had come to an end, and with it another Christmas separated from his family. This time they were not able to visit him until 29th December, but what a wonderful hour they shared together, and what tokens of love and consideration they provided in the many gifts they took for him; tangible evidence of goodwill to sustain him in the days ahead.

1st January, 1944. "Abreast another milestone in the march of time. May God grant that the new year bring peace on earth and relief to suffering humanity."[40] The following day he received the news he had waited so long to hear. He was to be released at last, and on 5th January he was homeward bound.

We can only guess at the excitement which accompanied his packing and preparations for release. The farewells which had to be said to those remaining; the friends he had shared so many experiences with during the previous three years. Some he had only come to know at Loveday, but others had shared Wayville and Tatura with him, and had become like a family in their shared moments of hope, sadness, and disillusionment. It seems likely that with the good news Schulz had received, their own hopes for release were also raised.

The wheels had been set in motion for Schulz's release as early as 21st July, 1943, when the Director General of Security had sent a statement to the Acting Attorney-General at Parliament House, Canberra, in which he remarked that the members of the Advisory Committee were experiencing "some difficulty in arriving at a decision, particularly in view of the weight of evidence given by a number of witnesses that the internee is a loyal British Subject".[41] The Director General considered this to be a 'borderline' case and suggested that the doubtfulness of Schulz's loyalty was enough to "warrant the continuation of his internment".[42] However, because Schulz was a natural born British Subject and because he, the Director General, had the delegated power to confirm any recommendation which the Advisory Committee decided to make, he had decided to submit the file for a Ministerial decision.

The Attorney-General, Dr. Evatt, considered the case and on 16th December, 1943, minuted the file in the following manner:

'I agree with D. G. S. that this is a borderline case: instead of reviewing it next February, I would suggest release of man (under restrictions) and review of behaviour in April 1944. In other words, release him on probation.'[43]

***

1. Federal Hansard, 7 September, 1939 p. 165.
2. Ibid, pp. 181 – 183.
3. AA: SA 18161 Loehe, Johannes Paul.
4. The Advertiser, 15 May, 1940.
5. AA: SA 20418 Lutheran Church.
6. Ibid.
7. AA: SS 1096 Major Sharland Personal 1943 - 1945.
8. Marie was his first grandchild.
9. Pastor Chris. Stolz was the son of Rev. J. J. Stolz, President of the U.E.L.C.A. Synod.

10. Hermann R. Homburg was a member of Parliament at the time of his arrest. He was interned on 25th November, 1940. He was released on 21st December after an appeal. He remained under open conditional arrest, which included having to move interstate. He was allowed to return to Adelaide in December, 1942. Refer to Ian Harmstorf's writing on Homburg in the Australian Dictionary of Biography.
11. J. F.W. Schulz, Diary entry, 13 December, 1940.
12. Fritz Homburg was born in Australia in 1887 of German parents. His father was a South Australian Judge. He was a brother to Hermann Homburg. Fritz was an Auctioneer and Estate Agent at Tanunda, and was considered a most prominent and influential member of the community. The Truth, 9 November, 1940, referred to him as the "uncrowned king" of Tanunda.
13. Copy of manuscript in author's possession.
14. J. F.W. Schulz, Diary entry, 11 January. 1941.
15. J. F.W. Schulz, Diary entry, 13 January, 1941.
16. The Truth, 5 Apr, 1941.
17. The Advertiser, 31 March, 1941.
18. J. F. W. Schulz, Diary entry, 22 January, 1941.
19. J. F. W. Schulz, Diary entry, 30 April, 1941.
20. J. F. W. Schulz, Diary entry, 2 May, 1941.
21. J. F. W. Schulz, Diary entry, 4 May, 1941.
22. Copy of letter in author's possession.
23. Copy of letter in author's possession.
24. Original manuscript in author's possession.
25. B. Patkin, The Dunora Internees, p. 112.
26. The 'Dunera' group had "fled Hitler's Europe only to be interned in England. Some of them had survived an attempt to ship them to Canada on the 'Arandora Star' ... which was torpedoed leaving 1200 people in the Irish Sea for good. Subsequently,

some of the 800 survivors, together with others were shipped to Australia on the 'Dunera' on which they were robbed by the later court-martialled guards ... In Australia they found them sitting between two chains on the floor. The British Government confessed its mistake. That Australian Government said they had never immigrated." Refer to the 'Dunera Internees', p. 137.

27. AA: AP 613
28. Ibid.
29. J. F. W. Schulz, Diary entry, 26-27 May, 1942.
30. J. F. W. Schulz, Diary entry, 12-25 April, 1942.
31. J. F. W. Schulz, Diary entry, 4-5 June, 1942.
32. Ibid.
33. AA: AP 613.
34. J. F. W. Schulz, Diary entry, 30 August, 1942.
35. AA: SS 827 J. F. W. Schulz.
36. J. F. W. Schulz, Diary entry, 26 January, 1943.
37. J. F. W. Schulz, Diary entry, 27-31 January, 1943.
38. J. F. W. Schulz, Diary entry, 25 April – 8 May, 1943.
39. AA: ACT A367.
40. J. F. W. Schulz, Diary entry, 1 January, 1944.
41. AA: ACT A367.
42. Ibid.
43. Ibid.

5

Release: What Happened to Schulz?

On 20th December, 1943, an Order Revoking Detention order and Imposing Restrictions as stipulated under the National Security (General) Regulations, directed that Schulz should accept employment offered to him through the Manpower Authorities and the Deputy Director of Security, in South Australia. Schulz would not be allowed to change his employment without prior permission from the Deputy Director of Security, and he had to reside at an approved address which was to be found for him by the authorities.[1] If this order had been promptly despatched, Schulz could have spent Christmas 1943 at home with his family. However, he was not notified of his release until two weeks later.

Following his release from 14D Internment Camp at Loveday, he was instructed to report to the Deputy Director of Security for South Australia, at 9 a.m. on Thursday, 6th January, 1944, where he was interviewed by Captain Sexton, Lieutenant Langford and Lieutenant Price.[2] The three men questioned him on Pan-Germanism, Die Bruecke, German visitors to South Australia, Dr. Becker, and a number of other persons who were interned. They also questioned him on his knowledge of the N.S.D.A.P. in Australia and Germany. Perhaps they thought that with his release assured he would suddenly be able to give them information which would fill in the gaps in the evidence provided against him. They possibly believed that the years of internment may have made him feel the need to prove his innocence by manufacturing the answers they wanted.

He was unable to provide them with the answers they wanted because there was little substance to their questions. Certainly, the N.S.D.A.P. had headquarters and members in Australia, but Schulz was unable to provide them with anything more than that he knew Becker was a member of this organisation. Since most of what they had in their files was based on hearsay, it would seem they needed something concrete to prove his internment was a valid move, particularly now the war was over and the hysteria was beginning to subside.

Although Schulz had been released, he was not a free man. He was restricted in his home life and in his contribution to the workforce. He was now under orders from the Manpower Authorities. The responsibility of the Security Service towards internees released under special orders was minimal. It was the duty of the Security Service to ensure that the type of employment was satisfactory from a security point of view. It was the duty of the Manpower Authorities to direct a person to employment after determining his physical fitness by means of a medical examination.

During the period 10th January to 5th May, 1944, Schulz was employed in various capacities and locations in Adelaide by the Manpower Authorities. These included Pope Products; Ford Brothers, Norwood; South Terrace Private Hospital; St. Peter's Girls School; S.A. Railway Car Sheds; Y.W.C.A., Hindmarsh Square; and General Motors Holdens, Woodville.[3]

Most of the work he undertook was in the capacity of handyman or cleaner. This was work he was not accustomed to. During March, while working as a handyman at South Terrace Private Hospital, Schulz injured his back through a fall down some stairs, and was allowed to return home prior to Easter to receive treatment from his own doctor.

Not only was Schulz finding difficulty working in various capacities for which he had not been trained, but the effect of constant moving around from one job to another was most unsettling. With each job move he invariably had to move to new accommodation, either in hotels or hostels.

His health, and that of his wife, was also a cause for concern. His wife could walk only with the aid of a walking stick as she suffered from an arthritic condition. During the cold weather she was forced to remain in bed for days at a time. Their daughter, Else, whose husband was on active service in New Guinea, lived at home and was nursing her mother. Else's husband was due for leave in May or June and Schulz knew the couple would be taking a holiday visiting relatives, which meant Schulz would have to find someone to attend to the care of his wife. The only solution appeared to be for Schulz to return home; work at Auricht's Printing Office doing clerical work, and care for his wife himself.

On 8th April, 1944, he wrote to the Deputy Director of Security, Mr. Kirkman, stating the problems he was facing and waited for a reply. He included in this letter the realization that at the end of April the State elections would take place and, in view of his connection with the last elections, he preferred to stay out of the district until the elections were over. During this time he was willing to do whatever work he was physically able to do in Adelaide.

On 24th April, 1944, permission for Schulz to return home at weekends was cancelled. The State elections were about to take place and once again the authorities decided not to take any chances with Schulz's influence in the Barossa Valley. A Memo regarding Schulz's application to return home, dated 10th June, 1944,[4] shows that some officials still showed an excessive amount of zeal in enforcing every aspect of the regulations.

The Deputy Director still considered Schulz to be a risk to the community. In his opinion Schulz's outlook and conduct had remained persistently the same for many years, and he found it impossible to say whether these views would persist if Schulz was allowed to return to his old associates and surroundings in "a thoroughly German district".[5] He considered it would be an extremely difficult task trying to keep a watch on Schulz's movements or connections, should he be allowed to live at home permanently.

In fact, it would have been a very easy task keeping track of his movements, given the number of informers who were still providing information on residents within the Barossa and surrounding districts. The Security Service of South Australia was receiving informers' reports on numerous residents of Tanunda on a weekly or fortnightly basis throughout 1944. One report for the week ending 3rd June, 1944 reads:

> 'Since my last reports Tanunda people and the district generally has quietened down to this extent that the people who were wont to express themselves rather freely are keeping more or less silent, until (I think) the election day is over. Mr. Richards, the Opposition Leader, expressly warned certain ones at the meeting at Baum's (referred to in Report No. 11) not to be — mugs, and to keep quiet so that the L.C.L. and its traitors could not have anything to charge them with. However, in spite of these warnings, these 'loyal' people never fail to express their views in no uncertain fashion to me on any possible occasion. I must confess

it gets heartily monotonous at times. However, every statement reported by me is actual fact and these people always speak with utter sincerity. Their loyalty does not exist, and although the war is turning against the man and the nation placed first in their hearts, their ardour and admiration, to say the least, never seems to cool. As an individual investigator from week to week I often wonder how these things can remain.[6]

The Deputy Director considered that if Schulz wanted to live with his wife he should make a home elsewhere. Fortunately, the Director General of Security, W. B. Simpson, appeared to be a thoughtful and considerate man, and after giving careful thought to Schulz's application decided to agree to Schulz's request, taking into consideration his age, state of health and that of his wife.

Schulz was duly informed. The conditions of his return were that he find work approved by the Manpower Authorities before he could return home. He immediately arranged to return to the family business, Auricht's Printing Office, at Tanunda. The authorities approved this and he returned to his home at last on 5th May, 1944.[7]

It was four years since he had been able to live permanently in his own home and share his life completely with his family, apart from those brief weekend visits in early 1944. He was an Australian born citizen who had not been found guilty of any crime, and though he was now able to live at home and work in his usual position as manager of a business, he was still under certain restrictions at the directive of the Manpower Authorities. And he was certainly still under observation by the Security Department, as can be seen from an informers report for the period 16-27 June, 1944.

'I arrived at Tanunda and visited J.F.W. Schulz who expressed pleasure at seeing me after our friendly relations while in the Internment camp ...'[8]

It was not until after the end of the war in 1945 that a Revocation of Restriction Orders was served on Schulz on 16th June, 1945. Finally he was a free man; his alleged crime against the country's security had been atoned for. But he still had unfinished business with the authorities. There were many loose ends to tie up and Schulz was not the kind of man to leave these undone. He wanted to know why he had been interned and he wanted his innocence acknowledged. He doggedly pursued the authorities over many issues, including the return of the film of von Luckner, which had been confiscated at the time of his arrest.

Schulz was finally given permission to collect the film from the Investigation Branch of the Attorney-General's Department in Adelaide on 8th July, 1946, together with papers from a Minute Book, and two small books dealing with Australian subjects which had been printed by Auricht's Printing Office. The Minute Book had been tendered as an exhibit before the Advisory Committee at Schulz's first hearing.[9]

Included in the package he collected was a small medal struck after the reign of Frederick August, King of Saxony, and a button or cap badge dated 1934, with the inscription in German, 'Outwards by its own strength'. The receipt of these two objects instigated another session of correspondence with the Investigation Branch, since they did not belong to Schulz. He was very curious as to how they came to be included in the package of things used in evidence against him. The authorities were unable to provide an answer to his question and were likewise unable to explain what had happened to Schulz's copy of Mein Kampf, which had not been returned to him.

In November of the same year, he wrote to the Hon. A.A. Calwell in Canberra, in an effort to solve the riddle. Part of the letter reads:

> 'The two badges or tokens in question mean nothing in themselves, but the fact that they were presented to the Tribunal which heard me is the serious point, when they were never my property. Is it not possible to ascertain when and by whom these exhibits were found in my possession? ... You will excuse me for continuing in my endeavours to clear my name. I owe it to my family to fight on.'[10]

Schulz rarely spoke about his internment with his family, but the driving force behind the continued correspondence with the authorities was his determination to prove his innocence. He wanted to set the record straight. He had been detained "for the safety of the Empire, and the successful prosecution of the war".[11] That is what hurt the most; the fact that he had been considered a threat to his fellow Australians.

The authorities, on the other hand, were becoming tired of his constant demands and considered that no good purpose would be served "by entering into what would certainly be a long, drawn out correspondence".[12] The suggestion was to inform Schulz that due to the length of time which had elapsed, it would now be impossible to trace the missing property, especially as many of the officers and other personnel responsible for the custody of internees property, were now dispersed throughout the Commonwealth.

Schulz made no further requests for the return of his property, but he did continue to pursue his burning desire to clear his name. He had asked "that a public pronouncement be made by the Prime

Minister as to the true reasons for the internment of persons against whom there was no suggestion of disloyalty".[13]

During May, 1947, the Attorney-General forwarded a letter regarding the numerous requests by Schulz to clear his name, to the Hon. A. A. Calwell, the Minister for Immigration and Information in Canberra. Part of the letter states:

> 'I have given some consideration to the representations made on behalf of Mr. Schulz and feel that the case does merit further enquiry even at this stage ... the matter might properly be referred informally to Mr. Justice Clyne who conducted the Australia First Inquiry and who himself has had experience of Committees in regard to internment.'[14]

There is no record of any further correspondence regarding Schulz's desire to clear his name or any ongoing considerations by the authorities, so one can only presume that Schulz finally gave up against the sheer weight of bureaucratic negativism. The authorities may have wished to sweep the whole issue, and others similar to Schulz's, under the carpet to save face. We may never know.

But Schulz's release and homecoming had had a happier side to it too. Apart from the joy of being back with his family, he was welcomed back with open arms by the majority of townsfolk. On his first day back at work he had decided to walk to Auricht's Printing Office, through the main street of Tanunda. People rushed out of shops to greet him and wish him well.[15] He was home; back where he belonged; a free man.

***

1. AA: ACT A367
2. Copy of Order in author's possession.
3. Copies of Official Directives in author's possession.
4. AA: ACT A367.
5. Ibid.
6. Ibid.
7. Copy of Official Directive in author's possession.
8. AA: SA 20418 Lutheran Church.
9. AA: SS 827 J. F. W. Schulz.
10. AA: ACT A367.
11. Ibid.
12. Ibid, Memo from Attorney General's Dept. Canberra, 28th February, 1947.
13. Ibid, 27th May, 1946.
14. Letter sent to Schulz by the Hon. A. A. Calwell, 14th May, 1947 in author's possession.
15. Verbal information from member of Schulz family.

6

In Retrospect: A Summary of the Issues

Schulz was a victim of circumstance. He was detained and interned on evidence provided by informers who did not have to substantiate their claims in a court of law, and whose motives for informing were never questioned.

In a document issued prior to his arrest, much of the information listed as reasons for his arrest was incorrect. This document, a Recommendation for Ministerial Warrant for Restriction or Detention Order under Regulations 25 and 26 of National Security (General) Regulations,[1] which was issued at Keswick Barracks, included a birth certificate for a Johann Friedrich Wilhelm Schulz who was born at Frankton, in the district of Kapunda, on 30th November, 1891.[2] My grandfather was born in 1883.

In a precis of the case, it was stated that Schulz was a member of the Hitler Club at Tanunda; that he had acted as a reporter for Die Bruecke in South Australia; that he had attended a number of meetings of the Nazi Party in Adelaide and that he had printed anti-Jewish literature at Auricht's Printing Office. This information was incorrect.

The Recommendation for Detention submitted that Schulz was "connected with an enemy organisation being either the Nazi Party or an organisation of like ideals, being an organisation inimical to the interests of the British Empire".[3] The report claimed that the above allegation was supported by Schulz's "display of allegiance to Hitler and his cause; his interest in Germans and all things German; his association with Dr. J. H. Becker, a notorious Nazi and Confidential Agent of the N.S.D.A.P. in Australia; his making disloyal and pro-Nazi utterances.[4]

This information came from so-called 'reliable sources', none of whom were ever called upon at either of his Hearings to swear in court that the evidence against him was true. A later report, compiled by the authorities during his internment, appears to have considered him less of a risk than was originally supposed.

> *'Putting aside the conflicting evidence concerning his pro-German utterances, the motives for his energetic war effort, and the uncertain reports of his membership of a 'Hitler League' etc., it is apparent that Schulz was one of the Tanunda clique which was associated with Dr. Becker, entertaining visiting Germans and fostering pan-Germanism ... Amongst other things he was a member of ... the German Historical Society ... There is no proof that Schulz was ever a member of the A.O. of the N.S.D.A.P. or attended more than one meeting at the Vienna Cafe in 1934.*[5]

The Security Service regarded the South Australian German Historical Society as an extension of the German Club (S.A.A.D.V.), which they considered to be a Nazi organisation. They concluded that 'Historical' was the word which successfully disguised the society as purely cultural.[6]

Schulz took an interest in this Historical Society simply because his parents had come to settle in South Australia from Germany. Like so many other first generation Australians, he was naturally interested in his heritage. He was never a member of the German Club, although he did show his film of von Luckner there on 14th September, 1938, at the request of the Club Secretary, Mr. Bay. Schulz had gone to Parafield Airport with Becker to see von Luckner's arrival. He thought it would be a wonderful opportunity to get an interesting film. He was not the only one who filmed von Luckner's arrival; the local Press representatives also photographed the occasion.[7]

To the authorities, Schulz was guilty by association. He tried to maintain his cultural heritage at a time when monoculturalism was the norm. Prior to World War Two, migrants were expected to have new attitudes and to adjust to the Australian way of life. Nowdays we have a multicultural society where we encourage people to be proud of their cultural heritage.

We need to learn from the experiences of the German communities in South Australia during the two world wars; learn not only to accept the differences between the many cultures we now have in this State, but also to realize that others who may seem different have much to offer us. Our South Australian community is a melting pot of cultural values, which began to simmer with the arrival of the first settlers.

Schulz, and many other German descendants, may have been rather naive in thinking they could continue their duality of interests at a time when fear and suspicion were gathering momentum during the pre-World War Two years. But we cannot lay the blame entirely on their naivety. The Military and Government Authorities reacted in a manner which belies our legal heritage; that which grants us the right to be innocent until proven guilty.

1. AA: SS 827 J. F. W. Schulz.
2. Ibid.
3. Ibid.
4. Ibid.
5. Ibid.
6. AA: SA 18743 German Historical Society of South Australia.
7. AA: SS 827 J. F. W. Schulz.

Illustration 8

Illustration 9

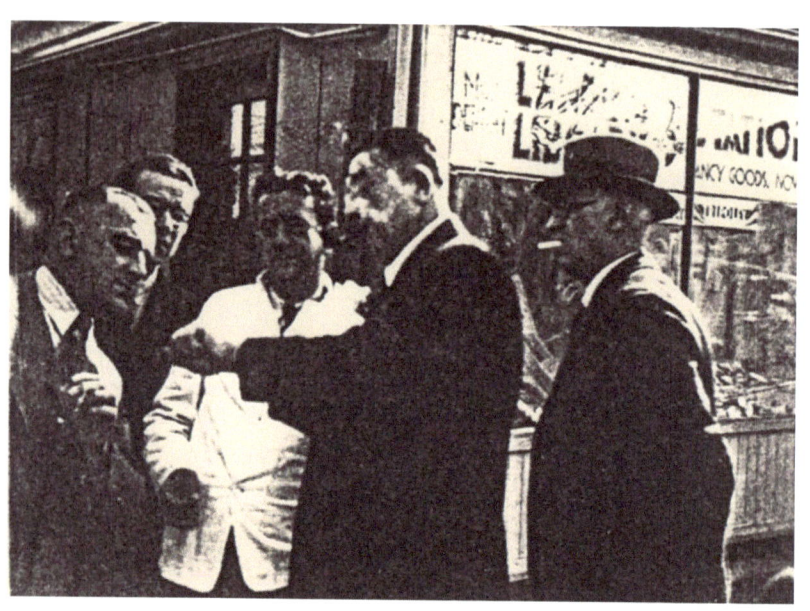

Illustration 10

Appendix A

Education Act Amendment Act.—1916.

Section 5.

THE SCHEDULE

GERMAN PRIVATE SCHOOLS TO BE CLOSED.

Name	Whether Proprietor or Head Teacher	Address	Name of School (if any)	Address of School House in which School held
W. Hoffmann	H.T.	Flinders Street, Adelaide	Martin Luther (Lutheran)	Flinders Street, Adelaide
Owned by congregation (Rev. O. Wiebusch)	—	Gawler	"	Allen's Creek (via Allendale North)
F. C. Hufner	H.T.	Australian Plains	Lutheran	Australian Plains
Carl Adolf Gerhard Dohler	H.T.	Pine Creek (Hun. of Appila)	"	Pine Creek (Hun. of Appila)
August Friedrich Hensel	H.T.	Bethany (near Tanunda)	"	Bethany (near Tanunda)
Martha Bruhl	H.T.	Bethel	"	Bethel
Ernest Paul Henry Schwarz	H.T.	(near Kapunda) Blumberg	"	(near Kapunda) Blumberg
B. Goedecke	H.T.	Bower	"	Bower
Marie Matuschka	H.T.	Crystal Brook West	"	Crystal Brook West
M. J. Backen	H.T.	Dalkey (near Balaklava)	"	Dalkey (near Balaklava)
Johannes Gottlieb Sangenschnitter	—	Dutton	"	Dutton
Robert Edwin Kernich	H.T.	Eden Valley	"	Eden Valley
Johanna Maria Wilhelmine Sperber	H.T.	Emmaus (near Eudunda)	"	Emmaus (near Eudunda)
Clara Liebel	H.T.	Emu Downs	"	Emu Downs
Wilhelm Paul Rekwmann	H.T.	Eudunda	St. Johns (Lutheran) Nain Lutheran	Eudunda
Hermann Adolph Heinrich	H.T.	Greenock	"	Greenock
Herman Paul Kempe	H.T.	Hahndorf	Lutheran	Hahndorf
Ernest O. F. Eckert	H.T.	Kapunda	Lutheran Trinity Lutheran	Kapunda
A. H. Vogelsang	H.T.	Killalpaninna	"	Killalpaninna
Otto Hubner	H.T.	South Kilkerran	St. Pauls	South Kilkerran
J. A. H. Gersch	H.T.	South Kilkerran	St. Johns	South Kilkerran
Benjamin Bernhardt Schwartzkopff	H.T.	Light's Pass	Lutheran	Light's Pass
Carl Eduard Brauer	H.T.	Lobethal	"	Lobethal
R. Kloeden	H.T.	Lower Bright	Martini Church	Lower Bright
Emilie M. Laske	H.T.	Lyndoch	St. Jakobi (Lutheran)	Lyndoch

GERMAN PRIVATE SCHOOLS TO BE CLOSED—*continued*.

Name	Whether Proprietor or Head Teacher	Address	Name of School (if any)	Address of School House in which School held
George Truss	H.T.	Mannum	Lutheran	Mannum
Johann Friedrich Jacob	H.T.	Moculta	"	Moculta
E. M. Isler	H.T.	Monarto	"	Monarto
Otto Gustav Hermann Hubner	—	Mount Torrens	Spring Head School (Lutheran)	Mount Torrens
J. G. Neumann	H.T.	Murray Bridge	Evangelistic Lutheran	Murray Bridge
Albert Rudolf Loerbel	H.T.	Neale's Flat	St. Johns	Neale's Flat
Alfred Gottlieb Kalms	H.T.	Neale's Flat	St. Pauls and St. Stephen Lutheran	Neale's Flat
Anna Maria Hulda Lehmann	H.T.	Neukirch (near Koonunga) New Residence	Evangelical (Lutheran)	Neukirch (near Koonunga) New Residence
Albert Conrad Mibus	H.T.	Nott's Well	Lutheran	Nott's Well
Emma Lydia Saegenschnitter	H.T.	North Rhine, Keyneton	"	North Rhine, Keyneton
Gustav Heinrich Otto Riedel	H.T.	Point Pass	Immanuel (Lutheran)	Point Pass
Heinrie's Albert Doecke	H.T.	Palmer	Lutheran	Palmer
Claas A. Brauer	H.T.	Peter's Hill (near Riverton)	"	Peter's Hill (near Riverton)
J. P. Eckert	H.T.	Rhine Villa	St. Johns (Lutheran)	Rhine Villa
Antonia Esther Nawk	H.T.	Rosenthal	St. Martin's	Rosenthal
J. R. Borman	H.T.	Robertstown	Lutheran	Robertstown
Theodor Bernhard Lossinas	H.T.	St. Kitts (near Truro) Springton	"	St. Kitts (near Truro) Springton
Christian Rorwedder	H.T.	Sedan	"	Sedan
Johann Alfred Edwin Dahlig	H.T.	Steinfeld (Hun. of Anna) Stockwell	Ebenezer	Steinfeld (Hun. of Anna) Stockwell
L. W. Zadow	H.T.	Tanunda	Langmeil	Tanunda
P. B. Zerna	H.T.	Carlsruhe (near Waterloo)	Lutheran	Carlsruhe (near Waterloo)
Paul Berthold Wilksch	H.T.			
J. F. W. Schulz	H.T.			
C. F. Beck	H.T.			

Adelaide: By authority, R. E. E. Rogers, Government Printer, North Terrace.

Appendix B

LIST OF 69 PLACENAMES OF GERMAN ORIGIN CHANGED BY THE NOMENCLATURE ACT OF 1917.

Bartsch's Creek to YEDLAKOO CREEK
Basedow, Hundred of to HUNDRED OF FRENCH
Bauer, Cape to CAPE WONDOMA
Berlin Rock to PANPANDIE ROCK
Bethanien to BETHANY
Bismarck to WEEROOPA
Blumberg to BIRDWOOD
Blumenthal to LAKKARI
Buchfelde to LOOS
Carlsruhe to KUNDEN
Ehrenbreistein to MT. YERILA
Ferdinand Creek to ERNABELLA CREEK
Mt. Ferdinand to MT. WARRABILLINNA
Friedrichstadt to TANGARI
Friedrichswalde to TARNMA
Gebhardt's Hills to POLYGON RIDGE
German Creek to BENARE CREEK
German Pass to TAPPA PASS
Germantown Hill to VIMY RIDGE
Gottlieb's Well to PARNGGI WELL
Grunberg to KARALTA
Grunthal to VERDUN
Hahndorf to AMBLESIDE
Hasse's Mound to LARELAR MOUND
Heidelberg to KOBANDILLA
Hergott Springs to MARREE
Hildesheim to PUNTHARI
Hoffnungsthal to KARAWIRRA
Homburg, Hundred of to HUNDRED OF HAIG
Jaenschtown to KERKANYA
Kaiserstuhl to MT. KITCHENER
Klaebes to KILTO
Klemzig to GAZA
Krause Rock to MARTI ROCK
Krichauff, Hundred of to HUNDRED OF BEATTY
Krichauff to BEATTY
Kronsdorf to KABMINYE
Langdorf to KALDUKEE
Langmeil to BILYARA
Lobethal to TWEEDVALE
Meyer, Mt. to MT. KAUTO
Muller's Hill to YANDINA HILL
Neudorf to MAMBURDI
Neukirch to DIMCHURCH
New Hamburg to WILLYAROO
New Mecklenburg to GOMERSAL
Oliventhal to OLIVEDALE
Paech, Hundred of to HUNDRED OF CANNAWIGRA
Petersburg to PETERBOROUGH
Pflaum, Hundred of, to HUNDRED OF GEEGEELA
Rhine Park to KONGOLIA
Rhine Hill to MONS
Rhine River N. to THE SOMME
Rhine River S. to THE MARNE
Rhine [North], Hundred of, to HUNDRED OF JELLICOE
Rhine [South], Hundred of, to HUNDRED OF JUTLAND
Rhine Villa to CAMBRAI
Rosenthal to ROSEDALE
Scherk, Hundred of, to HUNDRED OF STURDEE
Schoenthal to BOONGALA
Schomburgk, Hundred of, to HUNDRED OF MAUDE
Seppelts to DORRIEN
Schreiberhau to WARRE
Siergersdorf to BULTAWILTA
Steinfeld to STONEFIELD
Summerfeldt to SUMMERFIELD
Vogelsang's Corner to TEERKOORE
Von Doussa, Hundred of, to HUNDRED OF ALLENBY
Wusser's Nob to KARUN NOB

(By courtesy of Ian Harmstorf, Senior Lecturer in History at Adelaide College of Advanced Education.)

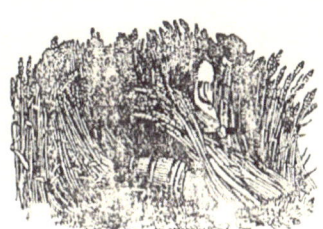

Appendix C

Appendix D

Appendix E

"Sowing Seeds"

Appendix F

Digging holes for foundation holes for hut posts

Appendix G

Ringing the gong for
"Smoke-Oh"

Appendix H

Back to work!

Appendix I

Erecting the electric light poles

Appendix J

7

Bibliography

Australian Government Records: Australian Archives S.A.

Security Service: Case Files Single No. Series A367 Item C66704 J. F. W Schulz.

Security Service: Case Files Single No. Series AP538/1 Item SA15320 Keller, Gustav Adolph.

Security Service: Case Files Single No. Series AP589/1 Item SS1550 German Historical Society of South Australia 1935-43.

Security Service: Case Files Single No. Series AP538 Item SA18743 German Historical Society of South Australia.

Security Service: Case Files Single No. Series AP538/1 Item SA20504 Immanuel College.

Security Service: Case Files Single No. Series AP538/1 Item SA22179 Basedow, Fritz Johannes.

Security Service: Case Files Single No. Series AP613 Item 130-1-7- P.O.W. and Internees Employment.

Security Service: Case Files Single No. Series CRSD1915 Item SA177 Riedel, Max Otto.

Security Service: Case Files Single No. Series CRSD1915 Item SA254 Lutheran Publications in German Language 1920.

Security Service: Case Files Single No. Series CRSD1915 Item SA334 German Propaganda 1920 only.

Security Service: Case Files Single No. Series CRSD1915 Item SA361 Goern, Hermann Otto Ernst.

Security Service: Case Files Single No. Series CRSD1915 Item SA406 Roehrs, Heinrich Friedrich Wilhelm 1915-1940.

Security Service: Case Files Single No. Series CRSD1915 Item SA1166 Lutheran Schools 1924-1925.

Security Service: Case Files Single No. Series CRSD1915 Item SA1679 Luckner, Count Felix 1927-1938.

Security Service: Case Files Single No. Series CRSD1915 Item SA2813 Homburg, Fritz 1916-1946.

Security Service: Case Files Single No. Series CRSD1915 Item SA6106 Stolz, J. J. 1943-1951.

Security Service: Case Files Single No. Series CRSD1915 Item SA11087 Alfred Freund—Zinnbauer.

Security Service: Case Files Single No. Series CRSD1915 Item SA15163 Dr. Johannes Heinrich Becker 1940-1948.

Security Service: Case Files Single No. Series CRSD1915 Item SA15196 Tummell, George 1916-1945.

Security Service: Case Files Single No. Series CRSD1915 Item SA17203 Visitors from Germany 1925-1939.

Security Service: Case Files Single No. Series CRSD1915 Item SA18121 German Club.

Security Service: Case Files Single No. Series CRSD1915 Item SA18161 Loehe, Johannes Paul.

Security Service: Case Files Single No. Series CRSD1915 Item SA19132 Krawinkel, Heinrich.

Security Service: Case Files Single No. Series CRSD1915 Item SA19561 Schrapel, Walter; Ernst; Aubrey; 1933-1941.

Security Service: Case Files Single No. Series CRSD1915 Item SA19620 Anti Semitism 1933-1942.

Security Service: Case Files Single No. Series CRSD1915 Item SA19631 Die Bruecke. German Australian Publications 1939-1945.

Security Service: Case Files Single No. Series CRSD1915 Item SA19641 Hermannsburg Mission 1919-1937.

Security Service: Case Files Single No. Series CRSD1915 Item SA19908 Internees, List of. 1940-1942.

Security Service: Case Files Single No. Series CRSD1915 Item SA20029 Fortbildungsverein (German Educational Society) 1934-1944.

Security Service: Case Files Single No. Series CRSD1915 Item SA20418 Lutheran Church.

Security Service: Case Files Single No. Series CRSD1915 Item SA20418/6 Some Aspects of the N.S.D.A.P. in Australia, South Australia 1943.

Security Service: Case Files Single No. Series CRSD1915 Item SA20419 Nazi Party in South Australia.

Security Service: Case Files Single No. Series CRSD1915 Item Security SA20502 New Guinea Missions 1937—1946.

Security Service: Case Files Single No. Series CRSD1915 Item SA21861 Queensland Herald.

Security Service: Case Files Single No. Series CRSD1915 Item SA21864 German Foreign Institute 1939-1945.

Security Service: Case Files Single No. Series CRSD1915 Item SA21865 Bund of Germans Abroad 1933-1945.

Security Service: Case Files Single No. Series CRSD1915 Item SA21866 German Winter Relief Fund 1936-1955.

Security Service: Case Files Single No. Series CRSD1915 Item SA22219 German Short Wave 1934—1939.

Security Service: Case Files Single No. Series CRSD1915 Item SA22367 Nationalist Activities in Germany after the War 1914-18.

Security Service: Case Files Single No. Series CRSD1915 Item SA23349 Homburg, Hermann Robert 1940—1954.

Security Service: Case Files Single No. Series CRSD1919 Item SS827 J. F.W. Schulz.

Security Service: Case Files Single No. Series CRSD1919 Item SS964 National Security (Manpower) Regulations 1942 only.

Security Service: Case Files Single No. Series CRSD1919 Item SS967 Non Enemy Internees 1941-1942.

Security Service: Case Files Single No. Series CRSD1919 Item SS971 P.O.W. and Internment Camps, Security of, 1942—1945.

Security Service: Case Files Single No. Series CRSD1919 Item SS972 Manpower Authorities, Information from 1942-1943.

Security Service: Case Files Single No. Series CRSD1919 Item SS988 Maps 1942-1944.

Security Service: Case Files Single No. Series CRSD1919 Item SS1004 Internments 1942-1943.

Security Service: Case Files Single No. Series CRSD1919 Item SS1010 Transfer of Internees 1942-1943.

Security Service: Case Files Single No. Series CRSD1919 Item SS1088 Reports on Internees 1943-1944.

Security Service: Case Files Single No. Series CRSD1919 Item SS1091 Employment of Ex Internees 1943-1944.

Security Service: Case Files Single No. Series CRSD1919 Item SS1095 Price, Charles A. 1946 only.

Security Service: Case Files Single No. Series CRSD1919 Item SS1096 Major Sharland Personal 1943—1945.

Australian Parliamentary Papers

Federal Hansard, 7 September, 1939.

Lutheran Archives

Church Register, Immanuel Lutheran Parish, Point Pass. S.A.

Mortlock Library

Shipping Register for 1881.

Private Papers (in author's possession)

J.F.W Schulz's diary: 13 December, 1940 to 5 January, 1944.

Bert Schulz's diary: 1936.

Copies of official documents relating to the internment of J. F. W. Schulz.

Private family letters.

Newspapers

The following were consulted:

The Sunday Times, Sydney, 23 November to 30 November, 1919.

The Advertiser, Adelaide, 15 May, 1940 to 31 March, 1941.

The Truth, Adelaide, 9 November, and 5 April, 1941.

Books and Pamphlets

Auricht's Almanac 1927, Auricht's Printing Office, Tanunda, S.A., 1927.

Borrie, W. D., Italians and Germans in Australia. A Study Of Assimilation, Angus and Robertson Ltd., Melbourne, 1954.

Christian Book Almanac 1933 (The), Lutheran Book Depot, U.E.L.C.A., North Adelaide, S.A. 1933.

Crowley, F. K., South Australian History. A Survey for Research Students, Libraries Board, Adelaide, S.A. 1966.

Dennis, B. E., Ethnic Development in South Australia, The Good Neighbour Council of S.A. Inc., 1972.

Gibson, M. & Zubrzycky, J., The Foreign Language Press in Australia 1848—1964, Australian National University Press, Canberra, 1967.

Harcus, W. (ed.), South Australia: Its History, Resources, and Productions, Government Printer, Adelaide, 1876.

Harmstorf, I. & Cigler, M., The Germans in Australia, AE Press, Melbourne, 1985.

Hebart, Th., The United Evangelical Lutheran Church in Australia (U.E.L.C.A.), Lutheran Book Depot, North Adelaide, 1938.

Homburg, H., South Australian Lutherans and Wartime Rumours, Adelaide, 1947.

Immanuel College Jubilee Souvenir 1895—1945. (Compiled by G. A. Keller.) College Jubilee Committee. (n.d.)

Internment in South Australia. Loveday Internment Group-Barmera. 1940-1946. (Compiled by Military Authorities and available in the State Library.) (n.d.)

Jensen, E., Barossan Foundations, Nuriootpa War Memorial Community Centre Committee Inc., 1969.

Leib, V.A, Grow Up To Christ. The History of a Lutheran School, Light Pass and Nuriootpa, S.A. 1846-1983. Redeemer Lutheran School, 1982.

Lutheran Church in Australia And Its Schools (The), Hunkin Ellis and King, Adelaide, 1920.

Lyng, J., Non Britishers in Australia, Melbourne University Press, 1935.

Patkin, B., The Dunera Internees, Cassell Australia Ltd., 1979.

Price, A. G., Founders and Pioneers of South Australia, Adelaide, 1929.

Price, C. A., German Settlers in South Australia, Melbourne University Press, 1945.

Sutherland, G., The South Australian Company. A Study in Colonization, Longmans, Green and Co., London, 1898.

Thiele, C., Barossa Sketch Book. Rigby, 1968.

Vansittart, R., Black Record: Germans Past and Present, Hamish Hamilton, London, 1941.

Whitelock, D., Adelaide 1836—1976. A History of Difference, University of Queensland Press, 1977.

Wilton, J. & Bosworth, R., Old Worlds and New Australia: the post war migrant experience, Penguin Australia, 1984.

Articles

Abbe, D. van, "The Germans in South Australia in Australian Quarterly, Vol. 28, No. 23, September 1956, pp. 69-75.

Abbe, D. van, "The Interests of the South Australian German-Language Press in the Nineteenth Century", in Historical Studies Australia and New Zealand, Vol. 8, No. 31, November 1958, pp. 319-321.

Harmstorf, I., "Homburg, Hermann Robert (1874-1964)", in Australian Dictionary of Biography, Vol. 9 pp. 355-356, Melbourne University Press, 1983.

Harmstorf, I., "Some Common Misconceptions about South Australia's Germans", in Journal of the Historical Society of South Australia, No. 1, 1975, p. 42.

Harmstorf, I., "They Worked Hard and Prayed Long", in The Bulletin, 10 July, 1976, p. 35.

Konig, W., "Internment in Australia", in Twentieth Century, Vol. 18, Spring 1963, pp. 4-21.

Price, C.A., "German Settlers in South Australia, 1838-1900", in Historical Studies Australia and New Zealand, Vol. 7, No. 28, May 1957, pp. 441-451.

Walker, R. B., "German Language Press and People in South Australia, 1848—1900" in Royal Australian Historical Society Journal, Vol. 58, part 2, 1972, p. 135.

Unpublished Theses

Harmstorf, I., "German Migration with particular reference to Hamburg, to South Australia 1851-1884. M.A. Thesis. University of Adelaide, 1971.

Miscellaneous

Bartrop, P., "'Military considerations take precedence over all others': refugees, enemy aliens and Australian Security, 1939-42." Unpublished paper presented at the Australian War Memorial History Conference, 11—15 February, 1985.

Bevege, M., "Internment in Australia in World War Two." Unpublished paper presented at the Australian Historical Association Conference, Melbourne University, August, 1984.

Harmstorf, I., "History of South Australian Tourist Districts. Barossa Valley. Part 3-Touring South Australia." Radio University Broadcast typescript, 7 October, 1974.

8

Tables, maps and illustrations

List of Tables

Table 1: German Immigration to S.A. 1861—1900.

Table 2: Applications for Naturalisation by Germans, S.A., 1848-1900.

Maps

Map 1: Central Prussia in 1844.

Map 2: The Barossa Valley.

Map 3: Distribution of persons of German birthplace in S.A. at Census of 1891.

Illustrations

Illustration 1: J.F.W. Schulz, or 'Mons' as he was known to his friends.

Illustration 2: J.F.W. Schulz at the beginning of his teaching career.

Illustration 3: Picking olives for the war effort, 1916 - J. F.W. Schulz and Tanunda Lutheran Day School children.

Illustration 4: Copies of Die Australische Zeitung on display outside Auricht's Printing Office, 1927 (J.F.W. Schulz at right)

Illustration 5: Published in The Sunday Times, Sydney, 23-11-1919. 'Tanunda, one of the many Hun centres of disloyalty in South Australia.'

Illustration 6: Monument erected on the Klemzig Cemetery Reserve in 1936.

Illustration 7: Count Felix von Luckner

Illustration 8: The Count and Countess von Luckner during their visit to the Barossa Valley.

Illustration 9: Dr. Becker (at left) and J. W. F. Schulz (at right) with von Luckner

Illustration 10: J.F.W. Schulz at work in Auricht's Printing Office during the 1950s.

9

Apendices

A: Education Act Amendment Act - 1916. German Private Schools To Be Closed.

B: List Of 69 Placenames Of German Origin Changed By The Nomenclature Act Of 1917.

C: J. F. W. Schulz at Loveday Camp – 'I get timber for a bed.'

D: J. F.W. Schulz at Loveday Camp — 'I make a bed for myself.'

E: J. F. W. Schulz at Loveday Camp — 'Sowing seeds.'

F: J. F. W. Schulz at Loveday Camp – 'Digging holes for foundation for hut posts.'

G: J. F. W. Schulz at Loveday Camp – 'Ringing the gong for Smoke-oh.'

H: J. F. W. Schulz at Loveday Camp – 'Back to work!'

I: J. F. W. Schulz at Loveday Camp – 'Erecting the electric light poles.'

J: J. F. W. Schulz at Loveday Camp – 'I am cook for the wood party.'

Liz Schulz by Maria Ames

Liz Schulz is an artist, educator, and author. The catalyst for the research that would become Prisoner Diaries and Guilty Till Proven Innocent was a request from Liz's mother more than 50 years ago. In 1970, on returning from living overseas for 10 years, her mother asked her to help research the Schulz family history. After she died 7 years later, the job of gathering together all the family documents fell to Liz. When she found the diaries, she knew they were an important part of not only her family, but Australia's social and wartime history.

As part of Liz's Bachelor of Education, she was encouraged by her professor, Margaret Allen, to research her grandfather's detention story. She researched the papers at the Australian Archives, and used content from her grandfather's diaries, family letters, and military documentation. After successful presentation and positive feedback, Liz sent copies to family members. Typed and bound, her copy languished on a bookshelf for decades.

When Liz retired in the mid-2000s, she chose the tranquillity of Andamooka in a semi-underground home built of local stone. She started sorting books and papers and came across the notebook where she had transcribed, in pencil, all his diary entries. Re-reading the papers provided her with the understanding that there was much more to tell.

Liz has wonderful memories of her grandfather and it feels like she is honouring him to tell his story and to share it as an example of detention, especially given Australia's current legislation.

Prisoner Diaries and Guilty Until Proven Innocent are dedicated to the memory of J.F.W. Schulz and Liz's twin sisters, Josie and Helen.

ABOUT THE BOOK

In 1940, Australian born, J.F.W. Schulz, a respected member of the community in Tanunda, South Australia, was arrested and put into detention. He was accused of being a Nazi and of keeping Nazi propaganda in his home. Although he maintained his innocence and made a number of appeals against his detention, he remained in detention, far from his family, for another three years and for a further year he was under government direction regarding his occupation and his place of residence.

In this meticulously researched history, his grand-daughter, Liz Schulz explores the reasons given for and the circumstances of his arrest. She had access to the security files of the Australian government: files which her grandfather was never able to examine. She was also able to draw upon her grandfather's own diary and correspondence held in private hands. In mapping his own quest for justice she seeks to get justice for her late grandfather.

While this thesis concerns one individual's struggle it also relates to wider issues about the rights of British subjects of German origin in war-time Australia. Furthermore it illuminates contemporary discussions about civil rights and the power of the state.

www.ingramcontent.com/pod-product-compliance
Lightning Source LLC
Chambersburg PA
CBHW042043290426
44109CB00001B/10